Florida Gators IQ:
The Ultimate Test of True Fandom

LARRY HORNE SR.

Printed in the United States of America.

Cataloging-in-Publication Data is available from the Library of Congress.

ISBN: 1449989470
First edition, second printing.

Cover photo courtesy of Christopher Rines.
Cover design by Holly Walden Ross.

Black Mesa Publishing, LLC
Florida

Black.Mesa.Publishing@gmail.com
www.blackmesabooks.com

Florida Gators

CONTENTS

INTRODUCTION

The University of Florida football program is a national power. No ifs, buts or doubts about it. It has become one of the elite.

The facilities, the coaches, players, administrative support and fans are among the finest anywhere. The Senior Class of 2009 has the most wins (48) in SEC history. But it's been a long journey – it didn't happen overnight. It was a gradual process with ups and downs. For sure, the journey has included a number of outstanding players and coaches.

The intent of this book is to refresh and rekindle your positive memories of some of the finest players and the coaches who have played such a significant role in helping make the University of Florida football program one of the finest in the country. All total, over 300 different players are mentioned in the six chapters and 300-plus questions in this book.

Gator Nation, sit back. Enjoy. Read this IQ book by yourself or with friends and family around the trivia table.

This is for you and Florida football fans everywhere around the country.

It's great to be a Gator!

1 BECOMING A NATIONAL POWER

"[Urban] Meyer's got such a handle on this thing that he beat half a dozen coaches this season who have National Championships on their resume. We're talking Bob Stoops, Nick Saban, Steve Spurrier, Bobby Bowden, Les Miles and Phil Fulmer . . . what he's built at Florida is scary good, and what he's building even more so."

— Dave George, Palm Beach Post Staff Columnist (10 January 2009)

Florida began its 2009 campaign as the overwhelming No. 1 team in the country, ahead of other powerhouse schools Texas, Oklahoma, Southern Cal, and Alabama.

It was the third time the Gators began a season on top of the AP poll, but with 58 of 60 possible first place votes the Gators claimed 96.7 percent of the votes – the highest percentage of first place votes for any preseason No. 1 in history.

Not bad, not bad at all.

NATIONAL CHAMPIONSHIPS

Question 1: The Gators won their first National Championship in what year?

a) 1965
b) 1966
c) 1996
d) 1998

Question 2: Who did the Gators defeat for their second National Championship?

a) UCLA
b) USC
c) Ohio State
d) Oklahoma

Question 3: The Gators won their third National Championship in 2008 after defeating these two teams, one for the SEC Championship and the other in the BCS Bowl for the National Championship.

a) Auburn and Ohio State
b) LSU and Ohio State
c) Alabama and Oklahoma
d) Alabama and Ohio State

Question 4: The Gators were undefeated in the SEC, including the SEC Championship Game, with a 9-0 record during this National Championship year. Which year was it?

a) 1965
b) 1996
c) 2006
d) 2008

Question 5: In which year did the Gators finish No. 3 in the AP poll but were recognized as the National Champion by *Sporting News* and the *New York Times*?

a) 1966
b) 1967

c) 1984
d) 1995

ANSWER KEY – NATIONAL CHAMPIONSHIPS

1. C – In 1996 the Gators defeated Florida State 52-20 in the Sugar Bowl to avenge a regular season loss to the Seminoles. The Gators finished No.1 in the AP and Coaches polls with a 12-1 record.

2. C – Ohio State. The 2006 Gators defeated Ohio State, 41-14, in the BCS National Championship Game. The Gators finished the 2006 season at 13-1.

3. C – Alabama and Oklahoma. In 2008 the Gators defeated Alabama, 31-20, for the SEC title and then beat Oklahoma in the BCS National Championship Game, 24-14. The Gators finished at 13-1.

4. B – 1996. The Gators ran the table in the SEC during the 1996 season with a 9-0 record, including a 45-30 win over Alabama in the SEC title game. Only a loss to non-conference rival FSU spoiled a perfect regular season. That loss, of course, was avenged in the Sugar Bowl to give the Gators the National Championship. In 1965 the Gators were 4-2 in the SEC. In 2006 and 2008 the Gators were SEC Champions with an 8-1 conference record both years.

5. C – 1984. The Gators finished the season at 9-1-1 but as stated in the question, two ranking systems had the Gators at No. 1 but the AP ranked the Gators at No. 3.

SEC CHAMPIONSHIPS

The Southeastern Conference (SEC) was founded in 1932. There were 13 original members of the SEC. They were the University of Alabama, University of Florida, University of Georgia, University of Kentucky; University of Mississippi; University of Tennessee; Auburn University; Louisiana State University; Mississippi State University; Vanderbilt University; Sewanee; Georgia Tech; and Tulane. These schools departed from the Southern Conference to establish their own conference. Sewanee, Georgia Tech and Tulane departed the SEC in 1940, 1964 and 1978, respectively. In 1992 the University of Arkansas and the University of South Carolina began play in the SEC and two divisions were created (West and East).

Question 6: When did the Gators win their first *official* SEC Championship?

a) 1966
b) 1967
c) 1991
d) 1993

Question 7: In 1993 the Gators won 28-13 in the SEC Championship Game in Birmingham, Alabama and set a then-school record of 11 wins with a victory vs. West Virginia in the Sugar Bowl. Who was their opponent in the Conference Championship?

a) LSU
b) Alabama
c) Arkansas
d) Mississippi

Question 8: In 2000 the Gators whipped up on this long-time rival in the SEC by the score of 28-6 in the SEC Championship Game. Who was the opponent?

a) LSU
b) Alabama
c) Auburn
d) Arkansas

Question 9: In 1994 the Gators narrowly beat (24-23) this SEC rival for its second consecutive SEC Championship (a first-time accomplishment).

a) LSU
b) Alabama
c) Arkansas
d) Mississippi State

Question 10: In 2008, Florida whipped this opponent (31-20) to win its eighth SEC Championship. Who was the opponent?

a) LSU
b) Alabama
c) Arkansas
d) Mississippi

ANSWER KEY – SEC CHAMPIONSHIPS

6. C – 1991. The Gators were undefeated in the SEC with a 7-0 record and 10-2 overall season record. It marked the first team to win 10 games in a season and it was the first team to have an unblemished record (no losses and no ties) in the SEC. The Gators would win their second SEC title in 1993 with an 8-1 mark. In 1966 and 1967 the Gators were 5-1 and 4-2, respectively, in the SEC.

7. B – Alabama. The 1993 team set a school record for the number of conference wins in a single season (8 - including the win in the SEC Championship game).

8. C – Auburn. The victory over Auburn gave the Gators another 10 win season and their sixth SEC Championship.

9. B – Alabama. The Championship made the Gators a dominating force in the SEC, as evidenced by two more SEC Championships in 1995 and 1996.

10. B – Alabama. In 2008, Alabama was No. 1 and Florida was No. 2.

MEMORABLE BOWL GAMES

Bowl game invitations did not become routine for the Gators until the 1990s. Since 1991 the Gators have appeared in a bowl game every year. The Gator Nation loves it!

Question 11: This Memorable Bowl game occurred when the Gators made their first appearance in a modern-day bowl, the 1952 Gator Bowl, and defeated their opponent, 14-13. The Gators finished at 8-3. Who did the Gators play?

a) Oklahoma
b) Oklahoma State
c) Tulsa
d) Rice

Question 12: This Memorable Bowl game was the Gators first *major* bowl win. The Gators defeated Georgia Tech, 27-12, on New Year's Day (January 1, 1967) which enabled the team to finish the 1966 season at 9-2. Name this major bowl.

a) Orange Bowl
b) Rose Bowl
c) Sugar Bowl
d) Cotton Bowl

Question 13: This Memorable Bowl game occurred when Florida won its first national title in 1996 by swamping Florida State, 52-20. The Gators finished at 12-1. What bowl was it?

a) Orange Bowl
b) Citrus Bowl
c) Sugar Bowl
d) Rose Bowl

Question 14: In this Memorable Bowl game Florida won its second national title in 2006 by thrashing this Big Ten opponent, 41-14, in the BCS National Championship Game. The Gators finished at 13-1. What Big Ten opponent did the Gators whip?

a) Michigan
b) Ohio State

c) Michigan State
d) Illinois

Question 15: In this Memorable Bowl game the Gators won their third national title in 2008 by soundly defeating this team, 24-14, in the BCS National Championship Game. The Gators finished at 13-1, matching the record of the 2006 team. Who did the Gators whip?
a) Oklahoma State
b) Oklahoma
c) Texas
d) Ohio State

ANSWER KEY – MEMORABLE BOWL GAMES

11. C – Tulsa.

12. A – Orange Bowl.

13. C – Sugar Bowl.

14. B – Ohio State.

15. B – Oklahoma.

MEMORABLE WINS (REGULAR SEASON)

Over the years there have been a number of "Memorable" games for the Gators as they have developed into a powerhouse football program. There is a tendency to make a game "more memorable" if you saw the game in person. And, of course, there have been many more than five memorable games – however, sit back and relive these games. They were undoubtedly special moments for the players, coaches and the Gator Nation.

Question 16: On September 25, 1954 the Gators (for the first time in Gator football history) beat a top-five ranked team. The final score was 13-12. Who was the opponent in this historic game?

a) Georgia
b) Georgia Tech
c) Clemson
d) NC State

Question 17: On October 12, 1963 the unranked Gators went on the road and beat this team, 10-6, which was ranked No. 3. Joe Namath was the opponent's quarterback. Who was the opponent?

a) South Carolina
b) Alabama
c) LSU
d) Auburn

Question 18: On October 29, 1966 the No. 7 ranked Gators beat this opponent 30-27 when quarterback Steve Spurrier kicked a 40-yard field goal with only 2:12 to play in the game at Florida Field. The extraordinary Homecoming win made the Gators 7-0. No doubt, this was a memorable game and memorable performance by the Gator quarterback who would become Florida's first Heisman Trophy winner. Who was the opponent?

a) Auburn
b) Alabama
c) Ole Miss
d) Mississippi State

Question 19: On November 1, 1986 the Gators topped this No. 5 team, 18-17. The Gators were down 17-0 in the fourth quarter which made this game one of the greatest comebacks in Gator history at Florida Field.

a) Auburn
b) Alabama
c) Ole Miss
d) Georgia

Question 20: On November 22, 1997 this opponent was ranked No.1 by two different polls and the Gators were ranked No. 10. The Gators scored a touchdown with 1:50 left in the game to win 32-29. As described by one long-time fan, "Every play was high drama." Who was the opponent?

a) FSU
b) Michigan
c) Georgia
d) Auburn

ANSWER KEY – MEMORABLE PLAYS (REGULAR SEASON)

16. B – Georgia Tech.

17. B – Alabama.

18. A – Auburn.

19. A – Auburn.

20. A – FSU.

MEMORABLE PLAYS (PART I)

Question 21: This Memorable Play (actually two plays) occurred on October 1, 1960. The Gators beat No. 10 Georgia Tech, 18-17, by scoring a TD and a two-point conversion with only 33 seconds left in the game. Who was the running back that scored the TD and who was the quarterback that tossed a wobbly pass to Jon MacBeth for the two-point conversion?

a) Lindy Infante (RB), Larry Libertore (QB)
b) Jim Rountree (RB), Larry Libertore (QB)
c) Rick Casares (RB), Jimmy Dunn (QB)
d) Hagood Clark (RB), Jimmy Dunn (QB)

Question 22: This Memorable Play occurred on September 20, 1969 when the Gators won this game by unleashing a passing attack against heavily favored Houston which was ranked No. 7. The final score was an amazing 59-34. On the third play of the game this sophomore duo for the Gators hooked up for a 70-yard TD pass. Name the quarterback and receiver.

a) John Reaves (QB), Carlos Alvarez (WR)
b) Steve Spurrier (QB), Charley Casey (WR)
c) Shane Mathews (QB), Charley Casey (WR)
d) Jimmy Dunn (QB), Carlos Alvarez (WR)

Question 23: This Memorable Play occurred on November 10, 1973. Behind 7-3 in the fourth quarter with no timeouts, this quarterback led a 13-play drive. The Memorable Play came on fourth and 18 when the Gator quarterback completed a pass to Lee McGriff for a TD. On the two-point conversion, the Gator quarterback tossed a bullet to tight end Hank Foldberg for the victory. Who was this quarterback that had several Memorable Plays on this winning drive to defeat Georgia, 11-10.

a) David Bowden
b) Don Gaffney
c) Jimmy Fisher
d) Terry LeCount

Question 24: This Memorable Play occurred on November 1, 1986 when an injured Gator quarterback came in off the bench to lead the Gators to victory in the fourth quarter. He "limped" into the end zone for a two-point conversion with only 36 seconds left to give the Gators an 18-17 victory.

a) Kerwin Bell
b) Bob Hewko
c) Rodney Brewer
d) Kyle Morris

Question 25: This Memorable Play came against LSU on October 7, 2006. The Gators had the ball on the one yard line with the score tied 7-7 with less than a minute to play in the first half . . . when the Gator quarterback faked a run, then jumped in the air and passed a one-yard TD pass to tight end Tate Casey. Gator fans could not believe what they had just witnessed. This quarterback would throw another TD pass and run for another TD. Who was the quarterback who performed this Memorable Play to lead the Gators to a 23-10 win?

a) Chris Leak
b) Tim Tebow
c) Ingle Martin
d) Noah Brindise

ANSWER KEY – MEMORABLE PLAYS (PART I)

21. A – Running back Lindy Infante (1960-62) and quarterback Larry Libertore (1960-62). Note: Jim Rountree (running back) played from 1955-57; Rick Casares (running back) played from 1951-53; quarterback Jimmy Dunn played from 1956-58; and, Hagood Clark (running back) played from 1961-63.

22. A – Quarterback John Reaves (1969-71) and wide receiver Carlos Alvarez (1969-71). Note: quarterback Steve Spurrier played from 1964-66; wide receiver Charley Casey played from 1963-65; quarterback Shane Mathews played from 1990-92; and quarterback Jimmy Dunn played from 1956-58.

23. B – Quarterback Don Gaffney (1973-75). Note: David Bowden was a Gator quarterback from 1972-73, Jimmy Fisher (quarterback) played from 1974-76 and Terry LeCount (quarterback) played from 1975-77.

24. A – Quarterback Kerwin Bell (1884-87). Note: quarterback Bob Hewko played from 1980-82; quarterback Rodney Brewer played from 1984-86; and Kyle Morris was a quarterback from 1988-90.

25. B – Quarterback Tim Tebow (2006-09). Note: Chris Leak (quarterback) played from 2003-06); Ingle Martin (quarterback and punter) played from 2002-03; and Noah Brindise (quarterback) played from 1995-97.

MEMORABLE PLAYS (PART II)

Question 26: This sophomore running back had a 94-yard TD run in the Orange Bowl following the 1966 season against No. 8 ranked Georgia Tech. The Gators won 27-12. This running back became an All-American.

a) Larry Smith
b) Emmitt Smith
c) Fred Taylor
d) Neal Anderson

Question 27: This Memorable Play occurred on November 12, 2006 against South Carolina. Ahead 18-17, the Gators blocked a field goal attempt by South Carolina as time expired in the game to preserve the victory. It was one of the great plays of the year because it kept the Gators in pursuit of a National Championship. Who was the defensive end of the Gators that blocked the field goal?

a) Carlos Dunlap
b) Ray McDonald
c) Jarvis Moss
d) Alex Brown

Question 28: This Memorable Play occurred on November 22, 1997 (See Memorable Wins). The opponent was ranked No. 1. Coach Steve Spurrier alternated quarterbacks Doug Johnson and Noah Brindise throughout the game. In the final seconds of the game Johnson completed a 63-yard pass to this outstanding receiver to set up two outstanding runs by running back Fred Taylor (the last one for the game-winning TD). Who was the receiver?

a) Travis McGriff
b) Jabar Gaffney
c) Ike Hilliard
d) Jacquez Green

Question 29: This Memorable Play occurred on September 11, 1993 at Kentucky. The Gators were behind, 20-18, when a redshirt freshman threw a 28-yard TD pass to sophomore receiver Chris Doering with three seconds to play to defeat Kentucky, 24-20. It was the start of this quarterback's career for the Gators which would culminate with the Heisman Trophy and a National Championship. Who was the quarterback?

a) Shane Mathews
b) Danny Wuerrfel
c) Kerwin Bell
d) Rex Grossman

Question 30: This Memorable Play occurred on January 8, 2009 in the BCS National Championship Game. With about 10 minutes to go in the game, this Gator defensive back intercepted a pass as Florida was clinging to a 17-14 lead over Oklahoma. The Gator defensive back actually swiped the ball from the receiver's hands for the interception to help the Gators win the National Championship, 24-14. Who is this defensive back that made one of the greatest Memorable Plays in Gator history?

a) Ahmad Black
b) Major Wright
c) Joe Haden
d) Reggie Green

ANSWER KEY – MEMORABLE PLAYS (PART II)

26. A – Running back Larry Smith (1966-68). Note: Emmitt Smith, an All-American, had 3,928 rushing yards from 1987-89 and had a 96-yard run against Mississippi State in 1988. Fred Taylor (1994-97), an All-American, ran for 3,075 yards and was a member of the 1996 National Championship team. Neal Anderson, an All-American, ran for 3,234 yards from 1982-85.

27. C – Defensive end Jarvis Moss (2005-06). Note: Carlos Dunlap (2007-09) was an outstanding defensive end who played on the 2008 championship team. Ray McDonald (2003-06) was a 1st Team All-SEC defensive end on the 2006 team. Alex Brown (1998-2000) was a 2nd Team All-American defensive end.

28. D – Wide Receiver Jacquez Green (1995-97). Note: Wide Receiver Travis McGriff (1995-98) was 1st Team All-SEC and third team All-American. Wide Receiver Jabar Gaffney (2000-01) was 1st Team All-SEC and 1st Team All-American. Wide Receiver Ike Hilliard (1994-96) was 1st Team All-SEC and 1st Team All-American.

29. B – Quarterback Danny Wuerrfel (1993-96). Note: quarterback Shane Mathews (1990-92) was 1st Team All-SEC and 2nd Team All-American. Quarterback Kerwin Bell (1984-87) was 2nd Team All-SEC and Honorable Mention All-American. Quarterback Rex Grossman (2000-02) was 2nd Team All-SEC and was drafted in the first-round of the NFL draft by the Chicago Bears.

30. A – Defensive back Ahmad Black (2008-09). Note: Defensive back Major Wright (2007-09) was an outstanding defensive back in both 2008 and 2009. Defensive back Joe Haden (2007-09) was a 1st Team All-American in 2009. Defensive back Reggie Green (1992-95) was another outstanding defensive back.

THE STREAKS

Question 31: The intense rivalry between the Gators and Florida State University began in 1958 with a Gator win, 21-7. What is the longest win streak (no ties and no losses) of the Gators against FSU?

a) 1965-66 (two consecutive wins)
b) 1958-60 (three consecutive wins)
c) 2004-09 (six consecutive wins)
d) 1968-76 (nine consecutive wins)

Question 32: In the 90s the Gators would enjoy a home winning streak that has not been matched since. How many games did the Gators win during this streak?

a) 24
b) 26
c) 30
d) 32

Question 33: In 2008 and 2009 the Gators set a new team record for consecutive wins. How many consecutive games did the Gators win?

a) 18
b) 20
c) 22
d) 24

Question 34: Name the first year that the Gators were undefeated and untied in the SEC (including the SEC Championship Game).

a) 1991
b) 1995
c) 1996
d) 2000

Question 35: Name the year of the Senior Class which is the "winningest" in SEC history.

a) Senior Class of 2006
b) Senior Class of 2007
c) Senior Class of 2008
d) Senior Class of 2009

ANSWER KEY – THE STREAKS

31. D – 1968-76 (nine consecutive wins).

32. C – 30. The Gators were unbeaten at home for 30 straight games beginning with a victory on October 29, 1994 and lasting until suffering defeat on October 2, 1999.

33. C – 22. The 2008 Gators won their last eight regular season games, the 2008 SEC Championship Game and the 2009 BCS Championship Game. The 2009 Gators won all 12 of their regular season games for a total of 22 consecutive wins.

34. A – 1991. The Gators were 7-0 in the SEC Conference.

35. D – Senior Class of 2009. This group of athletes won 48 games, lost only 7, won two National Championships and won two SEC Championships.

THE RIVALRIES (PART I)

The rivalries of the Gators have traditionally been Florida State, Georgia and the University of Miami. In recent years, the University of Tennessee, Louisiana State University and Auburn University have become somewhat intense games that have reached rivalry level. Miami is still considered a traditional rival although Florida and Miami did not play each other in 2009 because of their respective conference schedules.

Question 36: This rivalry is sometimes referred to as the "Battle for the Governor's Cup." The Gators have defeated this rival six consecutive seasons including a 37-10 win in 2009. Who is this rival?

a) University of Georgia
b) University of South Florida
c) Florida State University
d) University of Miami

Question 37: Since this rivalry began in 1958, the Gators have won 33, lost 19 and tied twice. Who is this rival?

a) University of Tennessee
b) Auburn University
c) Florida State University
d) University of Miami

Question 38: The festivities of this rivalry are sometimes referred to as the "World's Largest Outdoor Cocktail Party." Who is the opponent? The Gators have defeated this rival 17 times in the last 20 seasons, including a 41-17 win in 2009.

a) University of Georgia
b) Florida State University
c) University of Miami
d) University of Tennessee

Question 39: This game with an intense rival of the Gators is often referred to as the "third game of September" because that is the time frame that the game has usually been played since 1992. The 2001 game was rescheduled until later in the year because of the terrorist attack on September 11, 2001. In recent years this rivalry has become somewhat intense. Who is this rival?

a) Auburn University
b) Florida State University
c) University of Miami
d) University of Tennessee

Question 40: The rivalry with this non-SEC opponent dates back to 1938. The Gators defeated this key rival, 26-3, in their latest matchup which was played during the regular season in 2008. The Gators did not play this rival in 2009. Who is this rival?

a) Georgia Tech
b) Florida State University
c) University of Miami
d) Florida Atlantic University

ANSWER KEY – THE RIVALRIES (PART I)

36: C – Florida State University.

37: C – Florida State University.

38: A – University of Georgia.

39: D – University of Tennessee.

40: C – University of Miami.

THE RIVALRIES (PART II)

Question 41: This rivalry dates back to 1915 – almost 100 years ago. The game has been played in various locations including, Savannah, Tampa, Jacksonville, Athens and Gainesville. Who is this opponent?

a) University of Georgia
b) Florida State University
c) University of Miami
d) University of Tennessee

Question 42: This rival is a stiff competitor in the SEC Western Division. Including the Gators win over this top opponent in 2009, the Gators have a won-loss record of 31-23-3 over this top-notch team. Who is this opponent?

a) Mississippi State
b) Auburn University
c) Louisiana State University
d) University of Mississippi

Question 43: This SEC rival is in the same division (Eastern) as the Gators. The game has become intense and usually the winner of this game in the past few years has won the division and moved on to the SEC Championship Game. Who is this opponent?

a) University of Georgia
b) University of Tennessee
c) University of South Carolina
d) Vanderbilt University

Question 44: There were two games throughout the years that Gator fans will never forget in the history of Florida football against this SEC rival: (1) Steve Spurrier's field goal in the final seconds for a 30-27 win at Homecoming in Gainesville in 1966 and (2) the fourth-quarter comeback from a 17-0 deficit in 1986 when Kerwin Bell hobbled into the end zone for a two-point conversion (following his TD pass to Ricky Nattiel) for a 18-17 win. Name this SEC rival.

a) Mississippi State
b) Auburn University

c) Louisiana State University
d) University of Mississippi

Question 45: The Gators have defeated this rival five consecutive seasons including a 23-13 win in 2009. Who is this opponent?
a) Florida State University
b) University of Tennessee
c) Louisiana State University
d) University of Georgia

ANSWER KEY – THE RIVALRIES (PART II)

41. A – University of Georgia.

42. C – Louisiana State University.

43. B – University of Tennessee.

44. B – Auburn University.

45. B – University of Tennessee.

THE SWAMP

Question 46: When was the original construction completed of Florida Field? (It had a seating capacity of 21,769.)

a) 1920
b) 1930
c) 1940
d) 1950

Question 47: This Florida Head Coach coined the name "The Swamp." He was quoted as saying, "The Swamp is where Gators live." Can you name this outstanding coach?

a) Coach Ray Graves
b) Coach Charley Pell
c) Coach Steve Spurrier
d) Coach Urban Meyer

Question 48: The artificial surface, originally installed in 1971, was replaced in this year.

a) 1976
b) 1981
c) 1986
d) 1990

Question 49: Since 1950 what is the largest margin of victory for the Gators at home?

a) 46 points
b) 56 points
c) 66 points
d) 76 points

Question 50: The largest crowd to ever attend a Gator game at The Swamp was against this team (as of the end of the 2009 regular season).

a) University of Tennessee, 2009
b) University of South Carolina, 2006
c) Louisiana State University, 2006
d) Florida State University, 2009

ANSWER KEY – THE SWAMP

46. B – 1930. Note: The dedication of the field was on November 8, 1930 with Red Barber, a UF student at the time, providing the play-by-play. Red Barber would later become a famous broadcaster.

47. C – Coach Steve Spurrier.

48. D – 1990.

49. D – 76 points. The Gators walloped Central Michigan, 82-6, in 1997.

50. D – Florida State University, 2009. A record Ben Hill Griffin Stadium crowd of 90,907 attended the Gator-FSU game on November 28, 2009 – the final game of the 2009 regular season for the Gators. Note: The attendance beat the previous high of 90,894 attendance of the Florida-Tennessee game on September 19, 2009. The attendance for the Florida-South Carolina game in 2006 was 90,703. The attendance for the Florida-LSU game in 2006 was 90,714.

2 THE INDIVIDUAL AWARDS

"Florida's sophomore quarterback [Tim Tebow] thanked everyone he could think of, some of them twice. When it came time to take hold of the 25-pound bronze statue, he looked as if he wasn't sure whether he should run with the prize or throw it. He does both so well."
— Associated Press (8 December 2007)

"I love being a Gator, and I love Gator Nation."
— Tim Tebow, Heisman acceptance speech (8 December 2007)

Tim Tebow made history in 2007 when he became the first sophomore to claim the Heisman Trophy. He made history again in 2009 when he became the first player to be invited to the Heisman presentation for a third time.

Football is a team sport for sure, but Chapter Two is all about the Individual Awards – it's time to find out how much you know about your award-winning Gators.

THE FERGIE FERGUSON AWARD

The recipient of the Fergie Ferguson Award is selected by the coaches and is given to a senior who has demonstrated character, leadership and courage. As the name implies, the award is named in memory of Forrest K. "Fergie" Ferguson – a talented football player and leader who was an All-American for the Gators in 1941. He was seriously wounded in WWII (at Normandy) and died 10 years later from his wounds.

Question 51: All four of these players won the Fergie Ferguson award but which one was the first recipient of the award in 1954? He played in the backfield and was 2nd Team All-SEC in 1954.

a) Malcolm Hammock
b) Jim Rountree
c) Hagood Clarke
d) Larry Dupree

Question 52: This receiver won the Ferguson Award in 1965. He was a key receiver of many passes from quarterback Steve Spurrier in 1965 when he caught 58 passes to top the SEC. He was a two-time All-SEC selection and 1st Team All-American.

a) Sam Holland
b) Charles Casey
c) Richard Trapp
d) Lee McGriff

Question 53: This defensive player was awarded the Ferguson Award in 1972. He was 1st Team All-SEC and Honorable Mention All-American.

a) Fred Abbott
b) David Hitchcock
c) Steve Tannen
d) Mike Dupree

Question 54: This running back was selected for the award in 1985 when the Gators finished with a 9-1-1 record and a No. 5 ranking in the AP Poll. He was 1st Team All-SEC and Honorable Mention All-American. He later played for the Chicago Bears (1986-93).

a) James Jones
b) Neal Anderson
c) Rob Roberts
d) Ciatrick Fason

Question 55: This defensive player received the Ferguson Award in 1996 when the Gators won their first National Championship. He was 1st Team All-SEC.

a) William Gaines
b) Dwayne Thomas
c) Michael Gilmore
d) James Bates

ANSWER KEY – THE FERGIE FERGUSON AWARD

51. A – Malcolm Hammock. Note: Jim Rountree, Hagood Clarke and Larry Dupree received the award in 1957, 1963 and 1964, respectively.

52. B – Charles Casey. Note: Sam Holland, Richard Trapp and Lee McGriff received the award in 1962, 1967 and 1974, respectively.

53. A – Fred Abbott. Note: David Hitchcock, Steve Tannen and Mike Dupree received the award in 1973, 1969 and 1978, respectively.

54. B – Neal Anderson. Note: James Jones, Rob Roberts and Ciatrick Fason received the award in 1982, 2001 and 2004, respectively.

55. D – James Bates. Note: William Gaines, Dwayne Thomas and Michael Gilmore received the award in 1993, 1997 and 1994, respectively.

Note: Other winners of this prestigious award include Steve DelaTorre (1955), Larry Wesley (1956), Jimmy Dunn (1958), Asa Cox (1959), Pat Patchen and Vic Miranda (1960), Jim Beaver (1961), Jimmy Morgan (1963), Steve Spurrier (1966), Guy Dennis and Larry Smith (1968), Jack Youngblood (1970), John Reaves (1971), Jimmy Dubose (1975), Jimmy Fisher (1976), Wes Chandler (1977), Chuck Hatch (1979), David Little (1980), Brian Clark (1981), Dwayne Dixon (1983), Gary Rolle (1984), Ricky Nattiel (1986), Kerwin Bell (1987), Louis Oliver (1988), John Durden (1989), Kirk Kirkpatrick (1990), Cal Dixon (1991), Lex Smith (1992), Ben Hanks (1995), Willie Cohens (1998), Cheston Blackshear (1999), Jesse Palmer (2000), Byran Hardmon (2002), Daryl Dixon (2003), Jarvis Herring (2005), Jemalle Cornelius (2006), Andre Caldwell (2007) and Louis Murphy (2008).

THE JAMES W. KYNES AWARD

The James W. Kynes Award is presented annually to the offensive lineman who reflected the mental and physical determination and toughness as did Kynes himself, who was Florida's first All-SEC offensive lineman and was captain of the '49 Gators. This award began in 1986.

Question 56: The first recipient of this award also won the award two years later (1988). He was a second team All-American (Football News) and continued his playing career in the NFL with the Houston Oilers and New York Jets. Who was this outstanding offensive lineman?

a) David Williams
b) Bob Sims
c) Chris Bromley
d) Mark White

Question 57: This offensive tackle also won the Kynes Award two years – 1992 and 1995. He was an Honorable Mention All-American (Football News) in 1993. Who was this tackle?

a) Tony Rowell
b) Jim Watson
c) Anthony Ingrassia
d) Reggie Green

Question 58: This offensive guard won the Kynes Award in 1996 and helped the Gators win their first National Championship. He was a second team All-American (Football News).

a) Donnie Young
b) Zach Piller
c) Cooper Carlisle
d) Ryan Kalich

Question 59: This offensive tackle won the Kynes Award in 2000 and was a second team All-American.

a) Zac Zedalis
b) Mike Pearson
c) Bryan Savelio
d) Shannon Snell

Question 60: Two offensive linemen were honored in 2008 by sharing the Kynes Award. Name these two outstanding linemen.

a) Offensive tackle Jonathon Colon and offensive guard Lance Butler
b) Offensive tackle Steven Harris and offensive lineman Carlton Medder
c) Offensive lineman Phil Trautwein and offensive lineman Jason Watkins
d) Offensive guard Lance Butler and offensive lineman Jason Watkins

ANSWER KEY – THE JAMES W. KYNES AWARD

56. A – David Williams, offensive tackle. Note: Offensive guard Bob Sims, offensive guard Chris Bromley, and offensive tackle Mark White won the award in 1987, 1989 and 1990, respectively.

57. D – Reggie Green, offensive tackle. Note: Offensive tackle Tony Rowell, offensive guard Jim Watson and offensive tackle Anthony Ingrassia also won the award in 1991, 1993 and 1994, respectively.

58. A – Donnie Young. Note: Offensive tackle Zach Piller, offensive lineman Cooper Carlisle and offensive guard Ryan Kalich won the award in 1997, 1998 and 1999, respectively.

59. B – Mike Pearson. Note: Offensive lineman Zac Zedalis, offensive tackle Bryan Savelio and offensive guard Shannon Snell also received the award in 2001, 2002 and 2003, respectively.

60. C – Phil Trautwein and Jason Watkins. Note: Offensive tackle Jonathon Colon, offensive guard Lance Butler, offensive tackle Steven Harris and offensive lineman Carlton Medder also received the award in 2004, 2005, 2006 and 2007, respectively.

THE RAY GRAVES AWARD

The Ray Graves Award was initiated by a Gator coach who admired Coach Graves and highly respected him. The award was initiated in 1990 in tribute to Graves who coached from 1960-69 and compiled a 70-31-4 record. At the time, it was a record for the most wins in school history for a Head Coach. It is presented annually to the team's Most Valuable Player as selected by a vote of the team.

Question 61: Who was the Gator coach that originated the Ray Graves Award?

- a) Coach Galen Hall
- b) Coach Steve Spurrier
- c) Coach Bob Woodruff
- d) Coach Charlie Strong

Question 62: The first player to receive the Ray Graves Award was a tight end who was a 2nd team AP All-American selection in 1990. Who is he?

- a) Tony McCoy
- b) Kirk Kirkpatrick
- c) Ellis Johnson
- d) Mike Peterson

Question 63: This outstanding quarterback won the award in 1992 and continued his career with the Chicago Bears. Who is he?

- a) Shane Mathews
- b) Danny Wuerffel
- c) Rex Grossman
- d) Tim Tebow

Question 64: This outstanding running back for the Gators won the Ray Graves Award in 1993. He played pro ball for the Tampa Bay Buccaneers, Baltimore Ravens and Cleveland Browns. Who is he?

- a) Errict Rhett
- b) Fred Taylor
- c) Jeff Chandler
- d) Ciatrick Fason

Question 65: This safety won the award in 2006 and helped the Gators win the National Championship. He currently plays for the Jacksonville Jaguars. Who is he?

a) Carlton Miles
b) Jabar Gaffney
c) Keiwan Ratliff
d) Reggie Nelson

ANSWER KEY – THE RAY GRAVES AWARD

61. B – Coach Steve Spurrier (Head Coach 1990-2001).

62. B – Kirk Kirkpatrick (Tight end, 1990). Note: Defensive tackle Tony McCoy, defensive tackle Ellis Johnson and linebacker Mike Petersen won the Ray Graves Award in 1991, 1994 and 1998 respectively.

63. A – Shane Mathews (quarterback, 1992). Note: quarterback Danny Wuerffel won the award two times (1995 and 1996). Quarterback Rex Grossman won the award two times (2001 and 2002). Quarterback Tim Tebow also won the award in back-to-back seasons (2007 and 2008).

64. A – Errict Rhett (Running back, 1993). Note: Running backs Fred Taylor and Ciatrick Fason won the award in 1997 and 2004. Jeff Chandler was a place kicker who won the award in 1999.

65. D – Reggie Nelson. Note: Linebacker Carlton Miles won the award in 1992 along with quarterback Shane Mathews. Receiver Jabar Gaffney won the award in 2000. Cornerback Keiwan Ratliff won the award in 2003.

THE GATOR FOOTBALL RING OF HONOR

The Gator Football Ring of Honor is an award for the coach or athlete who has very distinctive qualities. While he must have been departed from the university for at least five seasons and must be in good standing with the university, he must meet at least one of the following characteristics: (1) Heisman Trophy; (2) Former Gator All American inducted into the NFL Hall of Fame for Accomplishments as a player; (3) Former Gator All-Americans who are NFL career category leaders; (4) College career category leader (5) Coaches with UF National Championships; (6) Coaches with at least three Gator SEC Championships; or (7) Players with two or more consensus All-American honors (AP, Walter Camp, Sporting News, AFCA, FWAA, UPI) who also were named National Offensive/Defensive Players of Year (AP, Walter Camp, Sporting News, ABC, AFCA, FWAA, UPI).

There are five Gator players who are members of the Gator Football Ring of Honor. Their names are familiar to you. In this category, you will get all five questions right . . . *right?*

Question 66: This running back was a unanimous 1st Team All-American selection. He finished seventh in the Heisman Trophy voting in 1989. An SEC Player of the Year in 1989, he broke 58 school records. Of course, he continued his stellar career with the Dallas Cowboys. Who is this very famous running back?

Question 67: This quarterback was an All-American and 1966 Heisman winner. Do we need to say more? Of course not – he was Mr. Everything as a player and came back as Head Coach to lead the Gators to the National Championship in 1996. Who is this very famous player and coach?

Question 68: This quarterback was the 1996 Heisman winner. Not much else needs to be said about this player either. He was a 1st Team All-American choice, completed 708 of 1,170 passes for 10,875 yards with 114 TD passes. Who is this very famous quarterback who led the Gators to their first National Championship?

Question 69: This All-American was a 1983 National Defensive Player of the Year. He was a finalist for the Lombardi Award in both his junior and senior seasons. He was a first-round draft choice of the Bears in 1984 and had an outstanding pro career. Who is this outstanding linebacker?

Question 70: This defensive end was one of the best-ever in Gator history. He became an NFL star for the Los Angeles Rams. He became the first player from the Gators to be inducted into the NFL Hall of Fame in 2001. Who is this well-known defensive end who played for the Gators from 1968-70?

ANSWER KEY – THE GATOR FOOTBALL RING OF HONOR

66. Emmitt Smith.

67. Steve Spurrier.

68. Danny Wuerffel.

69. Wilber Marshall.

70. Jack Youngblood.

THE COLLEGE FOOTBALL HALL OF FAME

The first class of College Football Hall of Fame inductees was selected in 1951 and included legends like Walter Camp, Jim Thorpe, Red Grange, Amos Alonzo Stagg and Knute Rockne. The College Football Hall of Fame is located in South Bend, Indiana.

Question 71: This College Football Hall of Fame inductee is probably the most famous running back in Gator history. In his junior season (1989) he rushed for 1,599 yards and finished his college career with 3,928 yards. He was named the Southeastern Conference Player of the Year and was selected to several All-American teams. He played for the Cowboys for several years. Who is this College Football Hall of Fame inductee?

Question 72: This Hall of Fame inductee was the National Defensive Player of the Year in 1983 and an All-American selection. He also was a professional player and a member of the Super Bowl Champions Chicago Bears (1985) and the Washington Redskins (1991). Who is this College Football Hall of Fame inductee?

Question 73: This Hall of Fame inductee was the first All-American for the University of Florida. He was an end for the Gators and he played from 1927-29. He was inducted into the Hall of Fame in 1975. Who is this College Football Hall of Fame inductee?

Question 74: This Hall of Fame inductee is one of the most famous of all Gator players. He was an All-American quarterback in 1966, played professional football and then returned to the Gators as Head Coach. He was inducted into the Hall of Fame in 1986 and he led the Gators to the National Championship in 1996. Who is this College Football Hall of Fame inductee?

Question 75: This Hall of Fame inductee is another one of the all-time great Gator football players. He was an All-American defensive end who played from 1968-70 and was inducted into the Hall of Fame in 1992. He was an NFL star for the Los Angeles Rams. Who is this College Football Hall of Fame inductee?

ANSWER KEY – THE COLLEGE FOOTBALL HALL OF FAME

71. Emmitt Smith.

72. Wilber Marshall.

73. Dale Van Sickel.

74. Steve Spurrier.

75. Jack Youngblood.

Note: Other College Football Hall of Fame inductees include Coach Ray Graves, Coach Charlie Bachman and Coach Doug Dickey. Coach Graves was Head Coach of the Gators from 1960-69. He was inducted into the Hall of Fame in 1990. Coach Bachman was Head Coach of the Gators from 1928-32. He was inducted in 1978. Coach Dickey was Head Coach of the Gators from 1970-78. He was inducted into the College Football Hall of Fame in 2003. He was also a quarterback for the Gators from 1951-53, although he was inducted into the Hall of Fame because of his coaching career.

THE HEISMAN TROPHY

The Heisman Trophy is a prestigious national award presented annually to the most outstanding college football player in the United States.

Note: In 2009, Florida quarterback Tim Tebow became the 20th recipient of the William V. Campbell Trophy, which honors college football's top scholar-athlete and is considered by many to be the "Academic Heisman." He joins former defensive tackle Brad Culpepper (1991) and fellow Heisman Trophy-winning quarterback Danny Wuerffel (1996) as Gator winners of the award. Florida now boasts the most recipients in the 20-year existence of the award.

Question 76: Three Gators have received the coveted Heisman Trophy – all quarterbacks – Steve Spurrier (1966), Danny Wuerffel (1996) and Tim Tebow (2007). How many other teams have had three quarterbacks to receive this prestigious award?

a) 3 other teams
b) 2 other teams
c) 1 other team
d) No other team

Question 77: Who was the outstanding Gator quarterback that placed a close second in 2001 for the Heisman Trophy? In fact, he was only 62 points short of winning the Heisman.

a) Shane Mathews
b) Rex Grossman
c) Chris Leak
d) Kerwin Bell

Question 78: Only four other schools in the nation have had more Heisman Trophy winners than the Gators. Name those four schools.

a) Notre Dame, Ohio State, USC and Oklahoma
b) Tennessee, USC, Georgia and Ohio State
c) UCLA, Notre Dame, Ohio State and Oklahoma
d) Michigan, Notre Dame, Ohio State and USC

Question 79: After Steve Spurrier won the Heisman in 1966, who was the first Gator to place in the top 10 voting for the Heisman? He was an outstanding All-American running back for the Gators in 1975 and he was sixth in the voting for the Heisman.

a) Jimmy Dubose
b) Nat Moore
c) Larry Smith
d) James Jones

Question 80: This All-American running back for the Gators placed in the top 10 voting for the Heisman two different years (1987 and 1989). He then played professional football for several years and set many records.

a) Emmitt Smith
b) Nat Moore
c) Larry Smith
d) James Jones

ANSWER KEY – THE HEISMAN TROPHY

76. C – one other team. Florida is one of only two schools in the nation with three quarterbacks to win the Heisman – the other school: Notre Dame.

77. B – Rex Grossman.

78. A – Notre Dame, Ohio State, USC and Oklahoma.

79. A – Jimmy Dubose.

80. A – Emmitt Smith. Note: Nat Moore (1972), Larry Smith (1968) and James Jones (1981) were also All-Americans for the Gators.

THE 1ST TEAM ALL-AMERICANS (1928-1970s)

Question 81: The Gators' first All-American (1st team) was a receiver who also played defense. He played on the 1928 team which went 8-1. After his career as a Gator, he became an outstanding stuntman for the motion picture industry.

a) Dale Van Sickel
b) Forrest "Fergie" Ferguson
c) Charlie LaPradd
d) Dennis Murphy

Question 82: This player was a 1st Team All-American guard in 1956 and the fourth All-American for the Gators.

a) Guy Dennis
b) Burton Lawless
c) Jack Youngblood
d) John Barrow

Question 83: This Gator was a tackle who played from 1956-58 and was the fifth All-American for the Gators.

a) Vel Heckman
b) Larry Gagner
c) Lynn Mathews
d) Bruce Bennett

Question 84: This outstanding player and leader was a 1st team All-American fullback in 1964. He was the team captain in '64 and grew up near Gainesville in Macclenny.

a) Charley Casey
b) Larry Dupree
c) Steve Spurrier
d) Bill Carr

Question 85: This tailback was a 1968 All-American for the Gators. He had a TD run of 94 yards against Georgia Tech in 1967 and later played in the NFL for the Los Angeles Rams and the Washington Redskins.

a) Steve Tannen
b) John Reaves
c) Larry Smith
d) Carlos Alvarez

ANSWER KEY – THE 1ST TEAM ALL-AMERICANS (1928-1970s)

81. A – Dale Van Sickel. Note: Fergie Ferguson was a two-way end and a star receiver for the Gators and was named an All-American in 1941. He set records which would stand from the early 1940s until the pro-style passing formations and plays two decades later. A Gator award is named after this heroic person who was the second Gator to be named a 1st team All-American. Charlie LaPradd was a popular All-American and one of the toughest linemen in Gator history. He played offense and defense. He was a member of the Gator's first bowl team. He later became president of St. Johns Community College in Palatka, Florida. Dennis Murphy (1962-64) was a 1st Team Football News All-American tackle in 1964.

82. D – John Barrow. Note: Guy Dennis was an All-American guard and offensive captain of the 1968 Gator team. Burton Lawless was a 1st Team All-American on the 1974 team. Jack Youngblood was a 1st Team All-American defensive end who played several years for the Los Angeles Rams. He is in the College Football Hall of Fame and the NFL Hall of Fame.

83. A – Vel Heckman. Note: Larry Gagner was a 1st Team All-American guard in 1965. He would play for Pittsburgh and Kansas City in the pros. Lynn Mathews was an All-American defensive end on the 1965 team. Bruce Bennett was a 1st team All-American defensive back in 1965 for the Gators. He played in the Canadian Football league for nearly a decade.

84. B – Larry Dupree. Note: Charley Casey was a 1st team All-American end for the Gators in 1965. Steve Spurrier was, of course, an All-American Heisman Trophy winner. Bill Carr was a 1st Team All-American for the 1966 team which included quarterback Steve Spurrier. In later years Carr would become the Athletic Director at the University of Florida.

85. C – Larry Smith. Note: Steve Tannen was 1st Team All-American defensive back in 1969 for the Gators. He played for the New York Jets in the NFL. John Reaves was a 1st Team All-American

quarterback in 1971. He played several seasons in the NFL and was a coach for Florida from 1990-94. Carlos Alvarez was a receiver for the Gators who was an All-American selection in 1969 when he caught 88 passes for over 1,300 yards and 12 TDs.

THE 1ST TEAM ALL-AMERICANS (1970s-1990s)

Question 86: This 1st Team All-American linebacker on the 1975 team started three seasons for the Gators. He played in the NFL with the Houston Oilers and the Seattle Seahawks.

a) Ralph Ortega
b) Sammy Green
c) Wes Chandler
d) Cris Collinsworth

Question 87: This linebacker for the Gators was an All-American in 1980. He became a starter for the Pittsburgh Steelers for many years. He has an older brother who was an All-Pro guard for the Miami Dolphins.

a) David Little
b) David Galloway
c) Wilbur Marshall
d) Lomas Brown

Question 88: This 1st Team All-American defensive back (1987) was also an All-SEC choice two consecutive years. He had 45 consecutive game starts – all four seasons. He played in the NFL for the Giants and the Dolphins.

a) Alonzo Johnson
b) Jeff Zimmerman
c) Clifford Charlton
d) Jarvis Williams

Question 89: This 1st Team All-American defensive tackle played only one year (1988) at Florida after transferring from Arizona State. He was a first-round draft choice of Chicago. He played for Chicago, Miami and Oakland.

a) Louis Oliver
b) Trace Armstrong
c) Emmitt Smith
d) Huey Richardson

Question 90: This tough running back made All-American honors in 1993. He completed his career with 4,163 yards rushing to beat

Emmitt Smith's rushing record. He was a second-round draft choice of Tampa and played in the NFL for several years.

a) Will White
b) Brad Culpepper
c) Errict Rhett
d) Judd Davis

ANSWER KEY – THE 1ST TEAM ALL-AMERICANS (1970s-1990s)

86. B – Sammy Green. Note: Ralph Ortega was an All-American linebacker in 1974. He played for the Atlanta Falcons and the Miami Dolphins. Wes Chandler was an All-American receiver in 1976 and 1977. He caught 92 passes in his career. He was an All-Pro receiver for the San Diego Chargers and NFL Wide Receiver of the Year in 1982. Cris Collinsworth was an All-American receiver for the Gators in 1980. He caught 120 passes for 1,937 yards and 14 TDs during his Gator career.

87. A – David Little. Note: David Galloway was an All-American defensive tackle in 1981. Wilber Marshall was an All-American outside linebacker for the Gators in 1982-83. He was an All-Pro selection for the Chicago Bears. Lomas Brown was an All-American offensive tackle in 1984 and then played for the Detroit Lions. He was an All-Pro selection for several years.

88. D – Jarvis Williams. Note: Alonzo Johnson was an outside linebacker who made All-American two consecutive years. He was a second-round choice of Philadelphia in the 1986 draft. Jeff Zimmerman was an All-American offensive lineman and has the distinction of being the first offensive lineman in Gator history to be named an All-American two seasons (1985-86). Clifford Charlton was a 1987 All-American outside linebacker and was a first-round draft choice of the Cleveland Browns.

89. B – Trace Armstrong. Note: Louis Oliver was a two-time All-American defensive back for the Gators in 1987-88. He was selected in the first-round of the 1990 NFL draft by Miami. Emmitt Smith is probably the most famous running back in Gator history. He was an All-American in 1989. He later played for the Dallas Cowboys and was the league MVP in 1993. Huey Richardson was an All-American defensive end in 1990. He was a four-time All SEC Academic Honor Roll choice.

90. C – Errict Rhett. Note: Will White was a free safety All-American choice in 1990 and was an All-SEC choice for three seasons. Brad Culpepper was an All-American defensive tackle in 1991. He played professionally for the Chicago Bears, Minnesota Vikings and Tampa Bay Buccaneers. Judd Davis was an All-American place kicker in 1993 who won the Lou Groza National Place Kicker Award.

THE 1ST TEAM ALL-AMERICANS (1990s-PRESENT)

Question 91: This 1994 defensive end was named to several All-American teams and was a finalist for the National Defensive Player of the Year Award. He also was an All-Pro defensive end for the St. Louis Rams in 1999.

a) Jack Jackson
b) Jason Odom
c) Kevin Carter
d) Danny Wuerffel

Question 92: This wide receiver was an All-American choice for the famed 1996 team that won the National Championship. In 1996 he caught 72 passes for 1,293 yards and 18 TDs.

a) Ike Hilliard
b) Reidel Anthony
c) Fred Weary
d) Jacquez Green

Question 93: This tailback was a 1st Team All-American choice in 1997 when he was the Gators leading runner with 1,292 yards on just 214 carries. The Jacksonville Jaguars chose him in the first-round and he played for the Jaguars for several years. He was an All-Pro selection in 2007.

a) Jevon Kearse
b) Mike Peterson
c) Fred Taylor
d) Alex Brown

Question 94: This quarterback was a 1st Team All-American in 2001. He also was a runner-up for the Heisman Trophy in 2001 and was named the National Player of the Year by the Associated Press. He was drafted by the Chicago Bears.

a) Jabar Gaffney
b) Rex Grossman
c) Mike Pearson
d) Keiwan Ratliff

Question 95: This tremendous athlete was a wide receiver who made All-American in 2007 and 2008. He was a double threat – as a receiver and running back. He completed his career with 32 touchdowns, 19 rushing and 13 receiving. He was the MVP of the 2006 SEC Championship Game.

a) Reggie Nelson
b) Percy Harvin
c) Aaron Hernandez
d) Brandon James

ANSWER KEY – THE 1ST TEAM ALL-AMERICANS (1990s-PRESENT)

91. C – Kevin Carter. Jack Jackson was an All-American wide receiver in 1994. He also was one of three national finalists for the Biletnikoff Award (the top receiver in the nation). Jason Odom was an All-American tackle in 1995. He was a starter for the Gators in 46 games and played professionally for the Tampa Bay Buccaneers. Danny Wuerffel was an All-American quarterback in 1995 and 1996; and, Heisman Trophy winner in 1996.

92. B – Reidel Anthony. Ike Hilliard was another All-American receiver on the '96 team. He had 47 receptions for 900 yards with 10 TDs in the Gators championship year. Fred Weary was an All-American defensive back for the 1997 Gators. He had 15 interceptions during his career and played for the New Orleans Saints from 1998-2001. Jacquez Green was an All-American selection in 1997. In 1998 he was a second-round draft choice by Tampa Bay.

93. C – Fred Taylor. Jevon Kearse was a 1st Team All-American selection in 1998 as a linebacker. He was the SEC Defensive Player of the Year and one of three finalists for the Butkus Award. He was a first-round draft selection by Tennessee. Mike Peterson was also an outstanding linebacker for the Gators in 1998. He was a 1st Team All-American choice in 1998 and was a second-round choice in the 1999 NFL draft by Indianapolis. Alex Brown was a 1st Team All-American in 1999 and 2001 as a defensive end. He was a finalist for the Lombardi Award in 2001.

94. B – Rex Grossman. Jabar Gaffney was a wide receiver who made 1st Team All-American in 2000 and 2001. He was a finalist for the Biletnikoff Award. He caught 27 TD passes during the 2000-01 seasons. Mike Pearson was an offensive tackle who also made 1st Team All-American in 2001. He was a second-round choice of Jacksonville in the NFL. Keiwan Ratliff was an outstanding cornerback for the Gators who was selected to nearly every All-American team in 2003. He was the SEC Defensive Player of the Year and was drafted by the Cincinnati Bengals.

95. B – Percy Harvin. Reggie Nelson was a 1st Team All-American safety in 2006. He was honored in 2006 by being selected as the recipient of the Vince Dooley Award as the nation's top defensive back. He was a first-round selection in the NFL draft by Jacksonville. Tim Tebow was named an All-American in 2007 and was the first sophomore to ever win the Heisman Trophy. Brandon James was selected an All-American in 2008 as a Special Teams player. He is an excellent return specialist.

THE NFL PLAYERS – FIRST-ROUND DRAFT PICKS

Question 96: Who was the first Gator player to be selected in the first-round of an NFL Draft? In 1945 this halfback was a first round selection of the Pittsburgh Steelers.

a) Paul DuHart
b) Roger Adams
c) Charlie LaPradd
d) Carroll McDonald

Question 97: Who was the second Gator player to be selected in the first-round of an NFL Draft? In 1950 this backfield player was a first-round selection of the Chicago Bears.

a) Chuck Hunsinger
b) James F. Dempsey
c) James W. Kynes, Jr.
d) Gaspar Vaccaro

Question 98: Who was the third Gator player to be selected in the first-round of an NFL Draft? He was drafted in 1967. This Gator was the third overall player selected and he played for the San Francisco 49ers from 1967-75 and the Tampa Bay Buccaneers in 1976.

a) Charley Casey
b) Steve Spurrier
c) John Reaves
d) Larry Gagner

Question 99: Who was the fourth Gator player to be selected in the first-round of an NFL Draft? This Gator was drafted in 1969 and was a running back. He was the eighth overall choice by the Los Angeles Rams. He played for the Rams from 1969-73 and the Washington Redskins in 1974.

a) Jim Yarbrough
b) Larry Smith
c) Nat Moore
d) Jimmy Dubose

Question 100: Who was the fifth Gator player to be selected in the first-round of an NFL Draft? This Gator was a defensive back and a 1st Team All-American in 1969. He was the 20th overall player chosen in the draft in 1970. He was drafted by the New York Jets and played for the Jets from 1970-74.

a) Jack Youngblood
b) Guy Dennis
c) Steve Tannen
d) Willie B Jackson

ANSWER KEY – THE NFL PLAYERS – FIRST-ROUND DRAFT PICKS

96. A – Paul DuHart. Note: Roger Adams was a center who was selected in the 24th-round of the 1946 draft by the Pittsburgh Steelers. Charlie LaPradd was a tackle who was drafted by the Green Bay Packers in the 25th-round of the 1952 draft. Carroll McDonald was a center who was drafted by the Green Bay Packers in the 13th-round of the 1952 draft.

97. A – Chuck Hunsinger. Note: James F. Dempsey was a tackle who was drafted in the 13th-round by the Chicago Bears. James W. Kynes, Jr. was a center who was drafted in the 14th-round by the Pittsburgh Steelers. Gaspar Vaccaro played in the backfield and was drafted in the 26th-round by the Pittsburgh Steelers. All three of these players were drafted in the same year as Hunsinger – 1950.

98. B – Steve Spurrier. Note: Charley Casey was an All-American receiver for the Gators. He caught 58 passes to top the SEC in 1965. He was drafted in the sixth-round by the Atlanta Falcons. John Reaves was a 1st Team All-American choice in 1971 who was drafted in the first-round by the Philadelphia Eagles. Larry Gagner played guard for the Gators and was drafted in the 15th-round in 1965 by the Cleveland Browns. He was a 1st Team All-American.

99. B – Larry Smith. Note: Jim Yarbrough was a tight end who was drafted in the second-round in 1969 by the Detroit Lions. Nat Moore was a running back for the Gators who was an Honorable Mention All-American choice in 1972. He was drafted by the Miami Dolphins in the third-round in 1974. Jimmy Dubose was a running back who was drafted in the second-round by the Tampa Bay Buccaneers in 1976. He was a second team All-American.

100. C – Steve Tannen. Note: Jack Youngblood was an All-American defensive end who was drafted in the first-round in 1971 by the Los Angeles Rams. Guy Dennis was a 1st Team All-American guard drafted in the fifth-round by the Cincinnati Bengals. Willie B. Jackson

was a receiver for the Gators who was drafted in the 11th-round in 1974 by the Los Angeles Rams.

Note: Other first-round draft selections throughout the years include: Glenn Cameron (1975), Wes Chandler (1978), James Jones (1983), Wilber Marshall (1984), Lomas Brown (1985), Lorenzo Hampton (1985), Neal Anderson (1986), John L. Williams (1986), Ricky Nattiel (1987), Clifford Charlton (1988), David Williams (1989), Louis Oliver (1989), Trace Armstrong (1989), Emmitt Smith (1990), Huey Richardson (1991), Ellis Johnson (1995), Kevin Carter (1995), Ike Hilliard (1997), Reidel Anthony (1997), Fred Taylor (1998), Mo Collins (1998), Jevon Kearse (1999), Reggie McGrew (1999), Travis Taylor (2000), Gerard Warren (2001), Kenyatta Walker (2001), Lito Sheppard (2002), Rex Grossman (2003), Jarvis Moss (2007), Reggie Nelson (2007), Derrick Harvey (2008) and Percy Harvin (2009).

3 THE POSITIONS

Percy Harvin won the AP 2009 NFL Offensive Rookie of the Year Award for the Minnesota Vikings. "I came in with an 'I'm ready for anything, I'm expecting anything attitude,' so nothing surprised me." You might say being a Gator is part of the reason Harvin carried that attitude to the NFL and helped his team earn a Division Title and a first-round bye in the playoffs during his first year in the league, in addition to winning top rookie honors.

After all, take a look at what the Gators have been producing at every position during the past few years according to the Gators 2009 Media Guide: all 13 seniors from the 2008 National Championship team graduated and earned a degree, 17 Gators have been selected in the NFL draft under Urban Meyer (and that's not including the 2010 draft), a nation high nine Gators were selected in the 2007 NFL draft, in the past four years there have been a total of 38 former Gators to sign a contract with an NFL team, and there have been four No. 1 draft picks from the Gators in the past four years.

You better believe it's great to be a Gator.

No question about it.

In Chapter Three it's time to look at each position on the gridiron and challenge yourself with questions about guys like Percy Harvin – guys who distinguished themselves in a specific role as a Florida Gator.

QUARTERBACKS

Question 101: In 2006 this senior quarterback guided the Gators to a 13-1 record, a SEC Championship and the National Championship.

a) Tim Tebow
b) Jesse Palmer
c) Rex Grossman
d) Chris Leak

Question 102: Who holds the record for the longest touchdown pass in Florida history? As a freshman backup quarterback, his TD pass of 99 yards against Rice in 1977 tied the NCAA record and set the Florida record. He became an All-American in 1980. However, not as a quarterback, but as a receiver. He also became a star receiver in the NFL.

a) John Brantley, Sr.
b) Cris Collinsworth
c) Charley Casey
d) Larry Rentz

Question 103: Who was the first Florida Gator quarterback to return to Florida as the Head Coach?

a) Steve Spurrier
b) Bobby Dodd, Jr.
c) Doug Dickey
d) Charley Pell

Question 104: Who is the quarterback that played for the Gators from 1965-67 and then became a very good running back for the Atlanta Falcons after his Gator career?

a) Tom Shannon
b) Larry Libertore
c) Harmon Wages
d) Jack Jones

Question 105: This Gator quarterback was a recipient of a 1977 Rhodes scholarship. Who is this Gator that achieved academic excellence and leadership?

a) Jimmy Dunn
b) John Reaves
c) Shane Mathews
d) Bill Kynes

ANSWER KEY – QUARTERBACKS

101. D – Chris Leak. Note: Tim Tebow (2006-09) was a freshman who saw valuable playing time behind senior Chris Leak. Tebow would be a Heisman winner as a sophomore and an All-American. He led the team to another National Championship in 2008. Jesse Palmer (1997-2000) was also an outstanding quarterback and would become a well-known sports commentator. Rex Grossman (2000-02) was an All-American quarterback who would be drafted by the Chicago Bears.

102. B – Cris Collinsworth. Note: Cris Collinsworth was moved to receiver in 1978. Collinsworth became an All-SEC selection for three years and an All-American his senior year. He played for the Cincinnati Bengals for several years and is now a nationally known sports commentator. John Brantley was a quarterback for the Gators in 1977-78. His son, John Jr., was the backup quarterback to Tim Tebow in 2008 and 2009. Charley Casey (1963-65) was a 1st Team All-American receiver for the Gators. Larry Rentz (1966-68) was the Gator quarterback in 1967 who threw a 52-yard touchdown pass to Richard Trapp and a 33-yard scoring pass to Mike McCann against Georgia for a 17-16 win.

103. C – Doug Dickey. Note: You may have been thinking Steve Spurrier on this one but not true. Spurrier was the second Gator quarterback to return to the Gators as Head Coach. Doug Dickey played quarterback for the Gators from 1951-53 and then returned as Head Coach from 1970-78. Spurrier played from 1964-66 and returned as Head Coach from 1990-2001.

104. C – Harmon Wages. Note: Harmon Wages was an outstanding athlete for the Gators. For most of his college career (1965-67) he was a backup to Steve Spurrier. He was a fine passer and an exceptional runner. He continued his career as a running back for the Atlanta Falcons and gained over 1,300 yards in five seasons. Tom Shannon was a quarterback for the Gators from 1962-64. Larry Libertore was a quarterback from 1960-62 and a 2nd Team All-SEC

selection in 1960. He was listed as weighing only 138-pounds. Jack Jones was a quarterback in 1959.

105. D – Bill Kynes. Note: Jimmy Dunn was a 142-pound starting quarterback for the Gators in the late '50s (1956-58). In 1969 sophomore John Reaves made his debut as the Gator quarterback. He quickly threw a 70-yarder to Carlos Alvarez for a TD against Houston. Reaves would throw for five TDs that day – a Gator victory, 59-34. He would receive Honorable Mention All-American honors as a sophomore and 1st Team All-American honors as a senior. Shane Mathews played from 1990-92 and was a 2nd Team All-American in his junior and senior seasons. He was 1st Team All-SEC all three seasons. Mathews played for the Chicago Bears and other teams in the NFL.

RECEIVERS

Question 106: This receiver led the Gators in receiving with 62 catches for 722 yards in 1992. He was a 1st Team All-SEC selection in 1992 and an Honorable Mention All-American in 1992-93. He was drafted by the Dallas Cowboys in the third-round of the NFL draft in 1994.

a) Wes Chandler
b) Jacquez Green
c) Reidel Anthony
d) Willie Jackson

Question 107: This receiver led the Gators in number of catches in 1959 with 14. He was a dual sport star (football and baseball) for the Gators. Other members of this athletically-gifted family have played football for the Gators.

a) Perry McGriff
b) Charley Casey
c) Richard Trapp
d) Dave Hudson

Question 108: This Gator wide receiver was honored with the National Football Foundation Scholar-Athlete Award in 1984 and a 1st Team Academic All-American in 1984.

a) Gary Rolle
b) Chris Doering
c) Erron Kinney
d) Jack Jackson

Question 109: This Gator receiver was a tight end who starred from 1980-82. He was drafted in the ninth-round of the NFL draft in 1983 by the San Francisco 49ers. He is the former coach of the Buffalo Bills and has been an assistant NFL coach for several years.

a) Mike Mularkey
b) Ricky Nattiel
c) Lee McGriff
d) Taylor Jacobs

Question 110: In one of the most famous games in Gator history, the Gators came from behind to defeat Auburn 14-10 in 1985 on an eight-yard pass from Kerwin Bell to this receiver with 7:18 remaining in the game for the win. That combination had scored earlier on a three-yard pass in the second quarter. The win enabled Florida to obtain its first No. 1 ranking in school history. Who is this receiver?

a) Reche Caldwell
b) Ray McDonald
c) Travis Taylor
d) Travis McGriff

ANSWER KEY – RECEIVERS

106. D – Willie Jackson. Note: Willie Jackson's father, Willie B. Jackson, played for the Gators from 1970-72. Wes Chandler had a dazzling 52-yard TD against Auburn in 1976 to help the Gators win, 24-19. He led the Gators in the number of receptions (a total of 92) for three consecutive years and was an All-American in 1976 and 1977. His average yards per catch (21.3) are the highest of any Gator. Jacquez Green (1995-97) and Reidel Anthony (1994-96) averaged 19.3 and 18.0 yards per catch respectively during their careers as outstanding Gator receivers.

107. A – Perry McGriff. Note: Charley Casey and Richard Trapp were outstanding receivers in 1963-65 and 1965-67 respectively. Casey was a 1st Team All-American. Trapp was a 1st Team All-SEC and Dave Hudson was a 1st Team All-SEC receiver (end) for the Gators from 1957-59. He was drafted by the Washington Redskins in 1960.

108. A – Gary Rolle. Note: Chris Doering (1993-95) was a 2nd Team All-American. Erron Kinney (1996-99) was a tight end who was selected in the third-round of the 2000 NFL draft. Jack Jackson (1991-94) was selected as a 1st Team All-American.

109. A – Mike Mularkey. Note: Ricky Nattiel (1983-86) was a 2nd Team All-American. He averaged 17.8 yards per catch during his career. Lee McGriff (1972-74) caught 36 passes for 698 yards in 1974 to lead the Gators. He was an All-SEC selection in 1974. Taylor Jacobs (1999-2002) led the team in receptions with 71 catches for 1,088 yards. He was 1st Team All-SEC.

110. B – Ray McDonald. Note: Reche Caldwell (1999-01) gained 1,059 receiving yards in 2001 to lead the team. He was a 2nd Team All-SEC in 2001. Travis Taylor (1997-99) was selected by the Baltimore Ravens in the first-round of the NFL draft in 2000. Travis McGriff (1995-98) was a 1st Team All-SEC selection and was selected in the third-round of the NFL draft by the Denver Broncos in 1999.

RUNNING BACKS

Question 111: This outstanding halfback for the Gators was an All-SEC selection for three consecutive years: 3rd Team in 1954 and 1955, and 2nd Team in 1956. He played both offense and defense – and he shares the longest interception return record in Gator history (100 yards, 1955 vs. Mississippi State).

a) Joe Brodsky
b) Rick Casares
c) Buford Long
d) Jackie Simpson

Question 112: This Gator running back of 1956 and 1957 was a fierce competitor and one of the best all-around athletes in Gator history. He was voted by the SEC coaches as the best blocker and tackler in the conference. He was on the Gator basketball and baseball teams as a freshman. He was drafted by the Reds and played professional football for the Cleveland Browns.

a) Bernie Parrish
b) Malcolm Hammock
c) Ed Sears
d) Chuck Hunsinger

Question 113: This Gator running back played a major role in helping the Gators have two of their most successful seasons of the '50s (1956 6-3-1, 1957 6-2-1). He was an All-SEC selection in 1956 (2nd Team) and 1957 (1st Team).

a) Jimmy Rountree
b) Dick Skelly
c) Robert Hoover
d) Bruce Starling

Question 114: This fullback was named SEC Player of the Year in 1975 by the *Nashville Banner* as selected by the league coaches. He ran for 1,307 yards for an average of 118.8 yards per game.

a) James Richards
b) Jimmy Dubose

c) Vince Kendrick
d) Robert Morgan

Question 115: This fullback played for the Gators from 1982-85 and was an Honorable Mention All-American selection (AP) in 1985. He was a first-round draft choice of the Seattle Seahawks. He played pro ball for 10 years and was named All-Pro two years.

a) Lorenzo Hampton
b) James Jones
c) John L. Williams
d) Earl Carr

ANSWER KEY – RUNNING BACKS

111. D – Jackie Simpson. Note: Joe Brodsky (1953-56) had two interceptions for TDs in the same game – vs. Mississippi State, 1956. He had a third interception in the same game but not for a TD. He was drafted by the Washington Redskins in 1957. Rick Casares (1951-53) was a 2nd Team All-SEC selection in 1952. He was drafted in 1954 by the Chicago Bears. He played in the NFL from 1955-64 and was a Pro Bowl selection two years. In 1956 he led the league in rushing with 1,156 yards. Buford Long (1950-52) was a 3rd Team All-SEC selection in 1952. He was drafted by the New York Giants in 1953.

112. A – Bernie Parrish. Note: Malcolm Hammock (1953-54) was a 2nd Team All-SEC in 1954 and was drafted in the third-round by the Chicago Cardinals. Reed Quinn (1951-52) was drafted in 1953 by the Pittsburgh Steelers in the 17th-round. Bill Dearing (1952-53) was drafted in 1955 by the Detroit Lions in the 29th-round.

113. A – Jimmy Rountree. Note: Dick Skelly (1960) was drafted in the third-round by the New York Giants. Robert Hoover (1960-62) was drafted in the ninth-round by the Minnesota Vikings. Bruce Starling (1960-62) was drafted in the 19th-round by the Denver Broncos.

114. B – Jimmy Dubose. Note: James Richards (1973-75) was selected in the seventh-round of the NFL draft by the New York Jets in 1976. Vince Kendrick (1971-73) was a running back for the Gators who was selected by the Atlanta Falcons in the fourth-round of the 1974 NFL draft. Robert Morgan (1974-76) was a running back for the Gators who was selected by the Tampa Bay Buccaneers in the 10th-round of the 1977 NFL draft.

115. C – John L. Williams. Note: Lorenzo Hampton (1981-84) was a running back for the Gators and was drafted in the first-round of the 1985 draft. James R. Jones (1979-82) was a 1st Team All-SEC selection in 1981-82 and 3rd Team All-American in 1982. He was selected in the first-round of the 1983 draft by the Detroit Lions.

Earl Carr (1975-77) was a Gator running back who was selected in the fifth-round of the NFL draft in 1978 by the St. Louis Cardinals.

OFFENSIVE LINEMEN

Question 116: This offensive lineman was selected as the recipient of the Jacobs Blocking Trophy in 2000 (presented to the SEC's top blocker as selected by the league coaches). He played for the Gators from 1998-2000. He was 1st Team All-SEC in 2000 and 2nd Team All-American as a tackle in 2000.

a) Kenyatta Walker
b) Mike Degory
c) Mac Steen
d) Steve DeLaTorre

Question 117: This offensive guard was selected as the recipient of the Jacobs Blocking Trophy in 1996. He was a 1st Team All-SEC choice in 1996 (another member of the '96 National Championship team) and a 2nd Team All-American.

a) Larry Gagner
b) Larry Beckman
c) Donnie Young
d) Burton Lawless

Question 118: This offensive lineman played for the Gators from 1983-86. He was a 1st Team All-SEC selection in 1985-86 and a 1st Team All-American in 1986. He was selected in the third-round of the 1987 NFL draft by the Dallas Cowboys.

a) Jeff Zimmerman
b) Phil Bromley
c) Jim Yarbrough
d) Mike Williams

Question 119: This center was selected as the recipient of the Jacobs Blocking Trophy in 1991. He was 1st Team All-SEC and 2nd Team All-American. An SEC Academic Honor Roll selection in 1991, he was picked in the fifth-round of the NFL draft by the New York Jets in 1992.

a) Carroll McDonald
b) Cal Dixon

c) David Williams
d) Kirk Kirkpatrick

Question 120: This offensive center was on the 1996 National Championship team and played from 1993-96. He was a 1st Team All-SEC selection in 1996. He also was a 3rd Team All-American. In 1997 he was selected in the fifth-round of the NFL draft by the Baltimore Ravens.

a) Mo Collins
b) Randy Jackson
c) Charlie Mitchell
d) Jeff Mitchell

ANSWER KEY – OFFENSIVE LINEMEN

116. A – Kenyatta Walker. Note: Mike Degory (2002-05) was an SEC Academic Honor Roll selection throughout his career as a Gator and a 1st Team All-SEC in 2005. Mac Steen (1967-69) was a 1st Team All-SEC in 1969. He was drafted by the San Diego Chargers in the 10th-round of the 1970 draft. Steve DeLaTorre (1952-55) was 1st Team All-SEC in 1955.

117. C – Donnie Young. Note: Larry Gagner (1963-65) was an offensive guard who made 1st Team All-SEC in 1964-65, and 1st Team All-American in 1965. He was chosen in the third-round by the Miami Dolphins (AFL). Larry Beckman (1964-65) 1st Team All-SEC in 1965. Burton Lawless (1972-74) was a 1st Team All-SEC in 1973-74. He was also 1st Team All-American in 1974 and drafted in the second-round by the Dallas Cowboys in 1975.

118. A – Jeff Zimmerman. Note: Phil Bromley (1981-84) was a center who was a 1st Team All-SEC in 1983-84 and a 2nd Team All-American in 1984. Jim Yarbrough (1966-68) was an outstanding tight end for the Gators who was drafted by the Detroit Lions in the second-round of the 1969 draft. Mike Williams (1973-75) was an offensive tackle who was 1st Team All-SEC in 1975 and an Honorable Mention All-American in 1975. He was chosen in the 13th-round of the 1976 NFL draft by the Atlanta Falcons.

119. B – Cal Dixon. Note: Carroll McDonald (1949-51) played center and linebacker. He was a 2nd Team All-SEC selection and played for the Detroit Lions. David Williams (1985-88) was an offensive tackle selected to the 1st Team All-SEC in 1988 and 2nd Team All-American in 1988. He was also drafted in the first-round by Houston in 1989. Kirk Kirkpatrick (1987-90) was a tight end who was a 1st Team All-SEC selection in 1990 and a 2nd Team All-American in 1990.

120. D – Jeff Mitchell. Note: Charlie Mitchell (1955-57) was an offensive tackle who was a 2nd Team All-SEC in 1957. Randy Jackson (1964-65) was an offensive tackle for the Gators who was

selected in the third-round of the AFL draft by the Buffalo Bills. He was also selected in the fourth-round of the NFL draft by the Chicago Bears. Mo Collins (1995-97) was an offensive tackle who was drafted in the first-round by the Oakland Raiders in 1998.

DEFENSIVE LINEMEN

Question 121: This defensive tackle was named the National Defensive Player of the Year for 1994 (by CNN). He was an All-SEC and an Honorable Mention All-American. He played for the Gators from 1991-94 and was credited with 36.8 total "tackles for loss" during his career. He was drafted by the Indianapolis Colts in the first-round of the NFL draft.

a) Marcus Thomas
b) Ellis Johnson
c) Mike Smith
d) Scott Hutchinson

Question 122: This defensive end was named the SEC Defensive Player of the Year by the AP in 2001. He was a 1st Team All-American and a fourth-round pick of the Chicago Bears in the 2002 draft. During his career with the Gators (1998-2001) he was credited with 46 total "tackles for loss."

a) Alex Brown
b) Ian Scott
c) Henry McMillan
d) Bobby McCray

Question 123: This defensive end was 1st Team All-SEC and an Honorable Mention All-American in 1969 for the Gators.

a) Tron LaFavor
b) David Barnard
c) David Ghesquiere
d) Darrell Lee

Question 124: This defensive tackle was a 1st Team All-SEC choice in 1991 and Honorable Mention All-American when he was credited with 17.5 total "tackles for loss." He was a fourth-round draft pick of the Indianapolis Colts in 1992.

a) Tony McCoy
b) Clint Mitchell
c) Gerard Warren
d) Reggie McGrew

Question 125: This defensive tackle was a 1st Team All-SEC selection in 1993 and a 3rd Team All-American in 1993 when he was credited with 14 total "tackles for loss." He was a sixth-round draft choice of the Miami Dolphins in 1994.

a) Joe Cohen
b) Derrick Harvey
c) Jarvis Moss
d) William Gaines

ANSWER KEY – DEFENSIVE LINEMEN

121. B – Ellis Johnson. Note: Marcus Thomas (2003-05) was selected to the SEC All-Freshmen team in 2003. He was a defensive lineman who played in 12 of 13 games and was credited with 47 tackles. Mike Smith (1973-75) was a defensive end who was drafted in the fourth-round by the Philadelphia Eagles in 1976. Scott Hutchinson was a defensive end who was selected in the second-round of the NFL draft by the Buffalo Bills in 1978.

122. A – Alex Brown. Note: Ian Scott (2000-02) was a 2nd Team All-SEC and 2nd Team All-American drafted in the fourth-round by the Chicago Bears in 2003. Henry McMillan (1992-94) was drafted in the sixth-round by the Seattle Seahawks in 1995. Bobby McCray (2001-03) was a 2nd Team All-SEC and a 2nd Team All-American drafted in the seventh-round of the 2004 draft by the Jacksonville Jaguars.

123. C – David Ghesquiere. Note: Tron LaFavor (1999-02) was drafted in the fifth-round in 2003 by the Chicago Bears. David Barnard (1992-95) was drafted by the Baltimore Ravens in 1996. Darrell Lee (2000-03) was drafted in 2004 by the Dallas Cowboys.

124. A – Tony McCoy. Note: Clint Mitchell (2000, 2002) was Honorable Mention All-SEC and Honorable Mention All-American. He was drafted in the seventh-round in 2003 by the Denver Broncos. Gerard Warren (1998-2000) was 2nd Team All-SEC. He was selected in the first-round of the 2001 NFL draft by the Cleveland Browns. Reggie McGrew (1996-98) was 1st Team All-SEC and was selected in the first-round of the 1999 NFL draft by the San Francisco 49ers.

125. D – William Gaines. Note: Joe Cohen (2003-06) was selected in the fourth-round of the NFL draft by the San Francisco 49ers. Derrick Harvey (2005-07) was a 2nd Team All-SEC and 2nd Team All-American selected in the first-round of the NFL draft in 2008 by the Jacksonville Jaguars. Jarvis Moss (2005-06) was selected in the first-round of the 2007 NFL draft by the Denver Broncos.

LINEBACKERS

Question 126: This outstanding linebacker spearheaded the great defense of the 2008 and 2009 teams. He was a 1st Team All-SEC and 1st Team All-American in 2008 and 2nd Team in 2009.

a) Brandon Spikes
b) Brandon Siler
c) Channing Crowder
d) Mike Nattiel

Question 127: This great linebacker was 1st Team All-SEC in 1978 and 1979. He also was an Honorable Mention All-American selection (two years). He had 467 tackles during his Gator career. He was chosen in the third-round of the NFL draft in 1980 and played eight seasons for the Tampa Bay Buccaneers. He has a nephew on the 2009-10 Gator team.

a) Scot Brantley
b) Mike Peterson
c) Mike Dupree
d) Patrick Miller

Question 128: This starting linebacker for the Gators in 1966 was a player who was "all-heart." He was listed as 158-pounds. He lettered for the Gators from 1964-66.

a) Fred Abbott
b) Jack Card
c) Glenn Cameron
d) Roger Pettee

Question 129: This 1985 1st Team All-American linebacker spearheaded the Gators defense. He played for the Gators from 1981-85. He had 11 sacks in 1984 and followed that up with 12 in 1985. He was a finalist for the Butkus Award in 1985. Drafted in the second-round by the Philadelphia Eagles, this linebacker played two seasons in the NFL.

a) Andra Davis
b) Ralph Ortega

c) Sammy Green
d) Alonzo Johnson

Question 130: This linebacker recorded 142 tackles during the 1992 season. He was 1st Team All-SEC and 1st Team All-American.
a) Ed Robinson
b) Byron Hardmon
c) Carlton Miles
d) Wilbur Marshall

ANSWER KEY – LINEBACKERS

126. A – Brandon Spikes. Note: Brandon Siler (2004-06) was 2nd Team All-SEC, 3rd Team All-American, and was drafted in the seventh-round of the NFL draft by the San Diego Chargers. Channing Crowder (2003-04) was 1st Team All-SEC, ESPN All-American and was drafted in the third-round of the 2005 NFL draft by the Miami Dolphins. Mike Nattiel (1999-02) was an Honorable Mention All-SEC and a sixth-round draft choice of the Minnesota Vikings.

127. A – Scot Brantley. Note: Mike Peterson (1995-98) was 2nd Team All-SEC, 1st Team All-American, and selected in the second-round of the NFL draft by the Indianapolis Colts. Mike Dupree (1976-78) was 2nd Team All-SEC and was selected in the seventh-round of the NFL draft by the Kansas City Chiefs. He had nine quarterback sacks his senior year. Patrick Miller (1982-85) was another outstanding linebacker for the Gators. He was drafted in the fifth-round of the NFL draft by the San Diego Chargers.

128. B – Jack Card. Note: Fred Abbott (1970-72) was 1st Team All-SEC, Honorable Mention All-American and was drafted in the sixth-round of the 1973 NFL draft by the Minnesota Vikings. Glenn Cameron (1972-74) was 1st Team All-SEC, 3rd Team All-American, and drafted in the first-round of the NFL draft by the Cincinnati Bengals. He had 185 total tackles during his Gator career. Roger Pettee (1962-64) was another outstanding Gator linebacker. He was drafted in the fifth-round by the Dallas Cowboys in the 1965 NFL draft.

129. D – Alonzo Johnson. Note: Andra Davis (1998-01) was 1st Team All-SEC, 2nd Team All-American and was drafted by the Cleveland Browns in the fifth-round of the NFL draft. Ralph Ortega (1972-74) was a 1st Team All-SEC, a 1st Team All-American and was drafted by the Atlanta Falcons in the second-round of the NFL draft. Sammy Green (1972-75) was 1st Team All-SEC, 1st Team All-American and a second-round draft choice of the Seattle Seahawks.

130. C – Carlton Miles. Note: Ed Robinson (1990-93) recorded 363 total tackles during his career as a Gator. He was an Honorable Mention All-American. Byron Hardmon (1999-02) recorded 168 tackles in a single season (2002). Wilbur Marshall (1980-83) is probably the best known linebacker in Gator history. He recorded 58 total "tackles for loss" during his career and recorded 27 tackles in 1981. He was 1st Team All-SEC and All-American.

DEFENSIVE BACKS

Question 131: This defensive back was named a 1st Team All-American and 1st Team All-SEC in 2009.

a) Joe Haden
b) Ahmad Black
c) Ryan Smith
d) Reggie Nelson

Question 132: This defensive back was named the SEC Defensive Player of the Year by the AP in 2003. He had three interceptions in one game (vs. Arkansas) and a total of nine interceptions for the 2003 season. Two of the interceptions were returned for touchdowns. He was a 1st Team All-American and All-SEC selection in 2003.

a) Lito Sheppard
b) Keiwan Ratliff
c) Fred Weary
d) Teako Brown

Question 133: This defensive back was one of the nation's highest honored athletes during 1993 and 1994. Both years he was a 1st Team Verizon Academic All-American selection. In 1994 he received the National Football Foundation and College Hall of Fame Scholar-Athlete Award.

a) Michael Gilmore
b) Tony Lilly
c) Will White
d) Louis Oliver

Question 134: This defensive back played from 1987-90 and had 10 career interceptions. He was one of 10 finalists for the Thorpe Award. He was a 2nd Team All-American and 1st Team All-SEC. He was an SEC Academic Honor Roll and was selected in the sixth-round of the NFL draft in 1991 by the Cincinnati Bengals.

a) Bruce Vaughn
b) Steve Tannen

c) Teako Brown
d) Richard Fain

Question 135: This defensive back was a 1st Team All-SEC and 1st Team All-American in 1965.

a) Larry Rentz
b) Bruce Bennett
c) Jim Revels
d) Wayne Fields

ANSWER KEY – DEFENSIVE BACKS

131. A – Joe Haden. Note: Ahmad Black (2008-09) was 2nd Team All-SEC in 2008 and 2nd Team All-Sophomore All-American selection by Football News. He had two interceptions for TDs. He also intercepted seven passes during the 2008 season which tied for the lead nationally. Reggie Nelson (2006) was 1st Team All-SEC, 1st Team All-American and one of three finalists for the Thorpe Award (presented to the nation's best defensive back). He was drafted in the first-round of the 2007 NFL draft by the Jacksonville Jaguars.

132. B – Keiwan Ratliff. Note: Renaldo Hill (2003-04) was selected in the seventh-round of the NFL draft by the Tennessee Titans in 2005. Lito Sheppard (1999-2001) was 1st Team All-SEC and 2nd Team All-American. He was selected in the first-round of the 2002 NFL draft by the Philadelphia Eagles. Fred Weary (1994-97) was a 1st Team All-SEC and 1st Team All-American. He was one of three finalists for the Thorpe Award and he was selected by the New Orleans Saints in the fourth-round of the 1998 NFL draft.

133. A – Michael Gilmore. Note: Tony Lilly (1980-83) was a 1st Team All-SEC and 2nd Team All-American in 1983. He was selected in the third-round of the NFL draft in 1984. Will White (1989-92) had 14 career interceptions and was 1st Team All-SEC in 1992. He was one of 15 finalists for the Thorpe Award. He was drafted in the seventh-round by the Phoenix Cardinals in 1993. Louis Oliver (1985-88) had 11 career interceptions and was a 1st Team All-SEC selection and 1st Team All-American in 1988. He was one of three finalists for the Thorpe Award. He was selected in the first-round of the NFL draft by the Miami Dolphins in 1989.

134. D – Richard Fain. Note: Bruce Vaughn played from 1980-83 and was an SEC Academic Honor Roll selection. Steve Tannen (1967-69) was a 1st Team All-SEC and 1st Team All-American in 1969. He was a first-round draft choice of the New York Jets. Teako Brown (1995-98) was 1st Team All-SEC in 1998.

135. B – Bruce Bennett. Note: Larry Rentz (1966-68) was not only a quarterback, (see quarterback section) he also was a defensive back and was drafted in the 17th-round of the NFL draft by the San Diego Chargers in 1969. Jim Revels (1971-73) was a defensive back who made 1st Team All-SEC and was drafted by the Miami Dolphins in the 12th-round of the 1974 draft. Wayne Fields (1972-75) made 2nd Team All-SEC in 1975 and was drafted by the Philadelphia Eagles in the 14th-round of the 1976 draft.

PUNT AND KICKOFF RETURN SPECIALISTS

Question 136: This Gator punt and kickoff returner played for the Gators from 1974-77. He also was a running back who rushed for 2,590 yards during his career as a Gator. He was the team leader for the 1974 season in All-Purpose yards with 1,115. He was a 1st Team All-SEC selection and was drafted by the Washington Redskins in 1978 in the sixth-round.

a) Tony Green
b) Cris Collinsworth
c) Reidel Anthony
d) Ivory Curry

Question 137: In 1993 this Gator returned a kickoff 100 yards to tie the SEC record and help the Gators defeat Mississippi State, 38-24. He also led the team for the 1994 season in All-Purpose yards with 1,287. He was 1st Team All-SEC and 1st Team All-American. He was selected in the fourth-round of the NFL draft by the Chicago Bears in 1995.

a) Pat Reen
b) Jack Jackson
c) Chuck Hunsinger
d) Harvin Clark

Question 138: In 1996 this Gator scored on back-to-back punt returns (66 and 79 yards) in a 65-0 win over Kentucky. He was an All-SEC and All-American selection in 1997. He was selected in the second-round of the 1998 NFL draft by the Tampa Bay Buccaneers.

a) Jacquez Green
b) Hal Griffin
c) Lito Sheppard
d) Steve Tannen

Question 139: In 1999 this Gator also returned a kickoff 100 yards to tie the SEC record and help the Gators defeat LSU, 31-10. He also had a kickoff return of 94 yards against Arkansas in 1997.

a) Tony Lomack
b) Reidel Anthony

c) Bo Carroll
d) Harrison Houston

Question 140: In 2008 this punt return specialist was named the SEC Special Teams Player of the Year by the AP. During the 2007 season he set an SEC record with a punt return average of 17.8 yards.

a) Loran Broadus
b) Ricky Nattiel
c) Keiwan Ratliff
d) Brandon James

ANSWER KEY – PUNT AND KICKOFF RETURN SPECIALISTS

136. A – Tony Green. Note: Cris Collinsworth (1977-80) had a 97-yard kickoff return against LSU in 1978. Reidel Anthony had a 90-yard kickoff return against Auburn in 1995. Ivory Curry (1980-82) had 631 yards in punt return yardage in his Gator career.

137. B – Jack Jackson. Note: Pat Reen (1938, 1940) had a kickoff return of 100 yards against Miami in 1940. Chuck Hunsinger (1948) had a kickoff return of 96 yards against Alabama in 1948. Harvin Clark (1969-71) had a kickoff return of 96 yards against Kentucky in 1969.

138. A – Jacquez Green. Note: Hal Griffin (1946-49) had a punt return of 97 yards against Miami (1946) and 87 yards against Villanova (1946). Lito Sheppard (1999-01) had two punt returns for touchdowns during the 2000 season. Steve Tannen (1967-69) had two punt returns for touchdowns during the 1968 season.

139. C – Bo Carroll. Note: Tony Lomack (1986-89) had a kickoff return of 99 yards against Kentucky in 1989. Reidel Anthony had a kickoff return of 90 yards against Auburn in 1995. Harrison Houston (1990-93) had an average of 22.5 yards per return during his career (54 for 1,019).

140. D – Brandon James. Note: Loran Broadus had a pair of 80-yard punt returns – one vs. Tulsa in 1948 and another vs. North Carolina in 1947. Ricky Nattiel (1983-86) had 346 yards (22 returns) in 1984. Keiwan Ratliff (2000-03) had a career punt return yardage of 860 yards.

PUNTERS

Question 141: This punter boomed an 82-yarder against Georgia in 1958 to set a record for the longest punt in Gator history. The record still stands. He averaged 44.9 yards a punt as a senior (another record for the Gators). After his Gator career, he was a punter for the Chicago Bears.

a) Hal Seymour
b) Bobby Joe Green
c) Buster Morrison
d) Don Chandler

Question 142: This punter of the 1960s was more known for his passes although he averaged over 40 yards per punt (130 punts) during his three-year career. He twice booted punts of 63 yards in 1964.

a) Steve Spurrier
b) Harry Spears
c) Jimmy Dunn
d) Don Ringgold

Question 143: This punter averaged 44.4 yards per punt during his four-year career as the Gator punter – the highest career average for a Gator. He had 161 total punts from 1982-85. He was drafted in the fifth-round by the Philadelphia Eagles in 1986.

a) Alan Williams
b) John James
c) Ray Criswell
d) Joe Borajkiewicz

Question 144: This punter has the longest punting average for a freshman in Gator history – 44.8 yards. He set the record in 2003. He also punted seven times for an average of 50.7 yards per punt against Georgia in 2003.

a) Eric Wilbur
b) Alan Rhine
c) Shayne Edge
d) Mark Dickert

Question 145: This outstanding punter averaged 43.4 yards per punt (44 punts) in 2008 and averaged 43.4 yards per punt (34 punts) in 2009.

a) Ingle Martin
b) Robby Stevenson
c) Jamie McAndrew
d) Chas Henry

ANSWER KEY – PUNTERS

141. B – Bobby Joe Green. Note: Hal Seymour (1964-65) was a punter for the Gators who averaged 40.7 yards per punt in 1963. Buster Morrison (1972-74) was a punter for the Gators who made the SEC Academic Honor Roll in 1972 and 1974. He booted a 66-yarder against FSU in 1974. Don Chandler (1955-56) was a great Gator punter who averaged 43.4 yards per punt. He also booted a 76-yard punt against Georgia Tech in 1955 which equals the second longest punt in Gator history.

142. A – Steve Spurrier. Note: Harry Spears (1953, 1956) averaged 38.1 yards per punt (34 punts) in 1956. Jimmy Dunn (1956-58) was a Gator quarterback who also handled the punting duties in 1957 – he averaged 33.2 yards per punt (28 punts). Don Ringgold (1960-61) averaged 39.6 yards per punt and 36.7 yards per punt.

143. C – Ray Criswell. Note: Alan Williams (1976-77) was selected by the New York Jets in the 12th-round of the 1978 draft. John James (1970-71) had a season average of 40.3 yards per punt for 57 punts in 1971. Joe Borajkiewicz (1981) punted for the Gators one year and had an average of 40.5 yards for 63 punts.

144. A – Eric Wilbur. Note: Alan Rhine (1999-2000) punted two years for the Gators and had a season high average of 43.3 for 65 punts in 2000. Shayne Edge (1991-94) booted a 76-yard punt against Vanderbilt in 1992 which equals the second longest punt in Gator history. He was the Gator punter all four years of his career and averaged 43.6 yards per punt his senior year. Mark Dickert (1980) had a punting average of 41.7 for 60 punts in 1980.

145. D – Chas Henry. Note: Ingle Martin (2002-03) booted a 70-yarder against Ole Miss in 2002 and finished that year with a 35.2 average for 46 punts. Robby Stevenson (1995-97) was the Gator punter for three years and his season high was 42.1 yards for 64 punts in 1969. Jamie McAndrew (1986-87) punted two years for the Gators and had a season average of 39.9 in 1987.

KICKERS

Question 146: This kicker holds the Gator record for the longest field goal – a 60-yarder which was booted in 1984 against Tulane. He is one of three players in SEC history with a 60-yarder. He made the SEC Academic Honor Roll in 1984.

a) Chris Perkins
b) Jeff Chandler
c) Wayne Barfield
d) Berj Yepremian

Question 147: This kicker won the Lou Groza National Place Kicker of the Year Award in 1993. He made 129 PATs out of 131 attempts during his career (1992-94) and completed his career with 81 consecutive PATs. He successfully booted 33 of 38 field goal attempts during his career.

a) Brian Clark
b) Judd Davis
c) John David Frances
d) Arden Czyzewski

Question 148: This field goal kicker successfully kicked the second longest field goal in Gator history – a 56-yarder against Georgia during the 2009 season.

a) Caleb Sturgis
b) Jonathan Phillips
c) Matt Leach
d) Bart Edmiston

Question 149: This kicker set the Gator record for most consecutive field goals in Gator history with 17 in 1984. He also made 43 of 49 attempts during his career (1982-84) as a Gator. He also holds the Gator record for total points scored by kicking in a single game (23) – six field goals and five PATs, set against FSU in 1983. Who is he?

a) Don Chandler
b) David Posey
c) Brian White
d) Bobby Raymond

Question 150: This kicker successfully booted two field goals in the final three minutes of a 19-17 win over Auburn in 1982. The first field goal was from 31 yards with 2:51 left in the game to bring the Gators within one point, 17-16. After a successful recovery of an onside kick, this Gator kicked a 42-yard game-winner with five seconds left on the clock.

a) Kendall Cook
b) Collins Cooper
c) Jim Gainey
d) Matt Piotrowiz

ANSWER KEY – KICKERS

146. A – Chris Perkins. Note: Jeff Chandler (1998-01) was a semi-finalist for the Lou Groza National Placekicker award in 1999 and 2000. He was drafted by the San Francisco 49ers in 2002. He was an Honorable Mention All-American. Wayne Barfield (1965-67) was a 1st Team All-SEC selection in 1967. He kicked a 31-yard field goal with 29 seconds remaining to defeat Georgia 17-16 in 1967. Berj Yepremian (1977-78) was a 2nd Team All-SEC selection in 1977.

147. B – Judd Davis. Note: Brian Clark (1979-81) made the SEC Academic Honor Roll in 1981 and was selected by the New England Patriots in the 10th-round of the NFL draft in 1982. John David Frances (1985-89) was a kickoff specialist and was a 2nd Team All-SEC selection in 1988. Frances also was an SEC Academic Honor Roll selection in 1989. Arden Czyzewski (1989-91) was a field goal kicker for the Gators and made 1st Team All-SEC in 1991.

148. A – Caleb Sturgis. Note: Jonathan Phillips (2005, 2008-09) set the Gator record of most PATs in a season (78) in 2008. He was a semi-finalist for the Lou Groza National Placekicker award in 2008. Matt Leach (2001-04) was a semi-finalist for the Lou Groza National Placekicker award in 2003. Bart Edmiston (1992, 1995-96) has the best perfect record of PATs in Gator history. He was 71 for 71 in 1995. He made the SEC Academic Honor Roll.

149. D – Bobby Raymond. Note: Don Chandler (1954-55) was a field goal kicker for the Gators and was drafted by the New York Giants. David Posey (1973-76) was selected in the ninth-round of the NFL draft by the San Francisco 49ers in 1977. He also made the SEC Academic Honor Roll in 1976. Place kicker Brian White (1992) made the SEC Academic Honor Roll in 1992.

150. C – Jim Gainey. Note: Place kicker Kendall Cook (1992-93) made the SEC Academic Honor Roll in 1992. Place kicker Collins Cooper (1996-98) made the SEC Academic Honor Roll in 1997. Matt Piotrowiz (2001-04) was a punter/place kicker who achieved All-SEC Academic Honors in 2002-03.

4 THE COACHES

It's a good feeling when your Head Coach is named Coach of the Decade by *Sporting News*. That would be Urban Meyer, of course, who was honored with that title in the fall of 2009. It's a much different feeling when just days prior to the Sugar Bowl that same coach announces he will be retiring due to health concerns.

If there is any question about why there was such an outpouring of emotion from Gator Nation over Meyer's decision, then perhaps it's worth considering the impact of his actions away from the gridiron – not the ones that earned him Coach of the Decade, but the ones with an even greater impact on individual lives.

Under Coach Meyer's leadership UF players now perform a minimum of 400 hours community service every year. They also attend a minimum of two "Goodwill Gator" events – per semester. In 2009, he opened up the "Swamp Field Trip" that saw local middle school kids given the opportunity to tour the stadium – with players as their hosts. The previous year he initiated the Gator Charity Challenge where football players hosted nearly 2,000 fans in a fundraising challenge that supported charities such as the American Cancer Society and the Susan G. Komen Breast Cancer Foundation, among others. That same year he created a mentoring program that partnered with 15 local middle schools "to affect change in the lives of at-risk black youth."

One of Meyer's former players, Vernell Brown, said, "If you're straight with coach, he's going to be straight with you. That's one of the best things about him. He's a guy who wants to know about you, talk to you, help you out." You can see the truth of Brown's statement in Meyer's relationships with his players – and it's a two-way street. Meyer's close relationship with Tim Tebow is well-documented, and it was Tebow's personal faith and commitment to missionary work that influenced Meyer to take his own personal commitment to his family, players, and community to a whole new level – which is why in the summer of 2008, Meyer and his family went on a missions trip to the Dominican Republic where they bought and served food for poverty stricken families.

Coach of the Decade, indeed.

And if you want to include what he's done on the field, well consider he's the first Florida coach to begin his career by beating Tennessee and Florida State five consecutive seasons, add two National Championships, a Heisman recipient, an impressive home record and even more dominant stats against other rival schools, and absolutely yes, it was hard for Gator Nation to absorb the shocking news that Coach Meyer was stepping down. It was Steve Spurrier who established Florida as a perennial powerhouse, but it was Urban Meyer who took it to a whole new level.

And then it was back . . . that good feeling again.

The sentiment was the same everywhere, fans were saying the right words – take care of your health and family first – but there was also a hollow ache, a bit of worry, wondering what's next. That's how it is in college football, because when you've got to replace the best, well . . . that means you're getting someone *less* than the best, right? And that is why there was such relief when Coach Meyer's retirement turned into a leave of absence, and now all signs point towards him being on the sideline in 2010.

Here's hoping for an exceptionally long and healthy Urban Meyer Era at Florida. In the meantime, Chapter Four is all about how we got to Urban Meyer. We start at the beginning and work our way forward – good luck!

THE START OF A FOOTBALL TEAM (1906-1949)

In 1906 the University of Florida's first football team was organized. The team finished its first season with a 5-3 won-loss record. The Florida team played such teams as the Gainesville Athletic Club, Rollins and Mercer.

Question 151: Who was the coach of that first team in 1906? He would also coach the Gators in 1907 and 1908. He compiled a record of 14 wins, 6 losses and 2 ties. Who would possibly know the answer to this question? Don't worry . . . the questions get easier as they get to the "Modern Era" of football, usually described as starting with the 1950 season.

a) Coach James Forsythe
b) Coach Charles J. McCoy
c) Coach Al Busser
d) Coach William Kline

Question 152: In 1913 the Gators beat Florida Southern 144-0 to record the most points ever scored by a Gator team. Can you imagine beating an SEC opponent by that score nowadays? Who was the Gator Head Coach in 1913? He was the second coach in Florida history and he posted a record of 26-7-3 in five seasons.

a) Coach Tom Sebring
b) Coach G.E. Pyle
c) Coach D.K. Stanley
d) Coach Josh Cody

Question 153: In 1928 and 1929 the Gators reached a new level when they were 8-1 and 8-2, respectively. Both seasons included wins over Georgia, Auburn and Clemson. Name the coach that headed up the Gators for five years (1928-32) which included these two very successful seasons.

a) Coach Charles Bachman
b) Major James Van Fleet
c) Coach Thomas J. Lieb
d) Coach Raymond B. Wolf

Question 154: During this season the Gators led the nation in scoring with 336 points in nine games. Hint: The Gators were led by All-American end Dale Van Sickel. Which season was it?

a) 1926
b) 1927
c) 1928
d) 1929

Question 155: Prior to joining the Southeastern Conference in 1933, what conference were the Gators in?

a) Big South Conference
b) Big East Conference
c) Big Eight Conference
d) Southern Conference

ANSWER KEY – THE START OF A FOOTBALL TEAM (1906-1949)

151. A – Coach James Forsythe. Note: Coach Charles J. McCoy was the Gator Head Coach from 1914-16. Coach Al Busser was the Gator Head Coach from 1917-19 and Coach William Kline was the Gator Head Coach from 1920-22. These coaches compiled records of 9-10, 7-8 and 19-8-2, respectively.

152. B – Coach G.E. Pyle. Note: Coach Tom Sebring was Head Coach from 1925-27. Coach D.K. Stanley was Head Coach from 1933-35. Coach Josh Cody was Head Coach from 1936-39. These coaches compiled records of 17-11-2, 14-13-2 and 17-24-2, respectively.

153. A – Coach Charles Bachman. Note: Major James Van Fleet was Head Coach from 1923-24. His record of 12-3-4 included an upset win over Alabama in 1923. Coach Thomas J. Lieb was Head Coach from 1940-45 (no team in 1943). His record was 20-26-1. Coach Raymond B. Wolf was Head Coach from 1946-49 and his record was 13-24-2.

154. C – 1928. The Gators scored 336 points and gave up only 44 points in nine games. The Gators were 8-0 going into their last game of the season, a 13-12 loss to Tennessee in Knoxville.

155. D – Southern Conference.

COACH BOB WOODRUFF (1950-1959)

Question 156: Coach Bob Woodruff was an alumnus of another SEC school and he played football at that school. What SEC school was it?

a) University of Alabama
b) University of Tennessee
c) University of Georgia
d) Louisiana State University

Question 157: What was Coach Woodruff's record at Florida, including postseason games, during his 10-year tenure?

a) 53 wins, 42 losses and 6 ties
b) 63 wins, 32 losses and 6 ties
c) 73 wins, 22 losses and 6 ties
d) 83 wins, 12 losses and 6 ties

Question 158: Coach Woodruff led the Gators to two bowl games. When were they?

a) 1952 and 1953
b) 1952 and 1957
c) 1952 and 1958
d) 1953 and 1958

Question 159: During Coach Woodruff's era, in what year did the Gators post their best record of 8 wins and 3 losses?

a) 1952
b) 1953
c) 1957
d) 1958

Question 160: What was the highest season-ending AP national ranking that the Gators achieved during Coach Woodruff's tenure?

a) No. 8
b) No. 14
c) No. 22
d) No. 24

ANSWER KEY – COACH BOB WOODRUFF (1950-1959)

156. B – University of Tennessee.

157. A – 53 wins, 42 losses and 6 ties.

158. C – 1952 and 1958 (both Gator Bowls).

159. A – 1952. The Gators were 8-3, including the Gator Bowl win over Tulsa.

160. A – No. 14. It came in the final AP Poll of 1958 with a 6-4-1 record. In terms of which season, if you were thinking 1952 it seems logical, but the 1952 Gators finished at No. 15 in the AP Poll.

COACH RAY GRAVES (1960-1969)

Question 161: Coach Ray Graves served as Head Coach of the Gators throughout the 60s, 1960-69. Like Coach Woodruff, he was an alumnus of another SEC school. He also played football at that school and was team captain his senior year. At what SEC rival of the Gators did Coach Bob Graves play football?

a) Alabama
b) Tennessee
c) Georgia
d) Louisiana State

Question 162: What was Coach Graves' record at Florida, including postseason games?

a) 60 wins, 41 losses and 4 ties
b) 70 wins, 31 losses and 4 ties
c) 80 wins, 21 losses and 4 ties
d) 90 wins, 11 losses and 4 ties

Question 163: During Coach Graves' era, in what year did the Gators post their best record of 9-1-1?

a) 1960
b) 1966
c) 1967
d) 1969

Question 164: How many bowl appearances did the Gators have during the 10-year era of Coach Ray Graves and how many were won?

a) 3 bowl games and 3 wins
b) 4 bowl games and 3 wins
c) 5 bowl games and 4 wins
d) 6 bowl games and 4 wins

Question 165: During Coach Graves' stint as Head Coach, what was the highest season-ending national AP ranking that the Gators achieved?

a) No. 10
b) No. 11
c) No. 12
d) No. 13

ANSWER KEY – COACH RAY GRAVES (1960-1969)

161. B – Tennessee. Like Coach Woodruff, Coach Graves also played football at the University of Tennessee.

162. B – 70 wins, 31 losses and 4 ties.

163. D – 1969. The Gators were 9-1-1. The next best records during the Graves era were 1960 (9-2) and 1966 (9-2).

164. C – 5 bowl games. The Gators won four of five bowl games during the Graves era: 13-12 over Baylor in the Gator Bowl in 1960; 17-7 over Penn State in the 1962 Gator Bowl; 27-12 over Georgia Tech in the Orange Bowl following the 1966 season and a 14-13 win over Tennessee in the 1969 Gator Bowl. The Gators lost to Missouri in the Sugar Bowl following the 1965 season.

165. B – No. 11. It came in the final AP Poll of 1966. The Gators won their first seven games of the season and finished at 9-2.

COACH DOUG DICKEY (1970-1978)

Question 166: Coach Doug Dickey served as Head Coach of the Gators from 1970-78. He was a college quarterback from 1951 through 1953. Who did he play for?

a) Alabama
b) Tennessee
c) Florida
d) Louisiana State

Question 167: What was Coach Dickey's record at Florida, including postseason games?

a) 58 wins, 43 losses and 2 ties
b) 68 wins, 33 losses and 2 ties
c) 78 wins, 23 losses and 2 ties
d) 88 wins, 13 losses and 2 ties

Question 168: During Coach Dickey's era, in what year did the Gators post their best won-loss record of 9-3 and finish second in the SEC with a 5-1 mark?

a) 1973
b) 1974
c) 1975
d) 1976

Question 169: How many bowl appearances did the Gators have during the nine-year era of Coach Dickey?

a) 3
b) 4
c) 5
d) 6

Question 170: During Coach Dickey's stint as Head Coach, what was the highest season-ending national AP ranking that the Gators achieved?

a) No. 14
b) No. 15

c) No. 16
d) No. 17

ANSWER KEY – COACH DOUG DICKEY (1970-1978)

166. C – Florida. Coach Dickey was a quarterback of the Gators from 1951-53, which included the Gator Bowl win over Tulsa, 14-13, in 1953.

167. A – 58 wins, 43 losses and 2 ties.

168. C – 1975. The Gators were 9-3, including a Sugar Bowl appearance. The SEC record of 5-1 was their best conference record since quarterback Steve Spurrier led the team to a 5-1 conference record in 1966.

169. B – 4. There were four bowl appearances by the Gators during the nine-year tenure of Coach Doug Dickey: the Tangerine Bowl in 1973 (a loss to Miami of Ohio, 16-7), the Sugar Bowl in 1974 (a 13-10 loss to Nebraska), the Gator Bowl in 1975 (a loss to Maryland 13-0), and the Sun Bowl in 1976 (a 37-14 loss to Texas A&M).

170. B – No. 15. It came in the final AP Poll of 1974 with an 8-4 record.

COACH CHARLEY PELL (1979-1984)

Question 171: Coach Charley Pell was the Head Coach of the Gators from 1979 through the first three games of 1984. Previously, he was the Head Coach at Clemson University. Similar to Coach Woodruff and Coach Graves, Coach Charley Pell also was an alumnus of another SEC school and he played football at that school. Where did Coach Charley Pell play college football?

a) Alabama
b) Tennessee
c) Georgia
d) Louisiana State

Question 172: What was Coach Pell's record at Florida, including postseason games?

a) 43 wins, 16 losses and 3 ties
b) 33 wins, 26 losses and 3 ties
c) 23 wins, 36 losses and 3 ties
d) 13 wins, 46 losses and 3 ties

Question 173: Coach Pell's greatest moment may have been the Gators 17-9 victory over this west coast power in 1982 which attracted national attention.

a) USC
b) UCLA
c) Washington
d) Oregon

Question 174: During the five-plus years of Coach Pell's era, in what year did the Gators post their best record of 9-2-1?

a) 1980
b) 1981
c) 1982
d) 1983

Question 175: During Coach Pell's era, what was the highest season-ending national AP ranking achieved by the Gators?

a) No. 6
b) No. 13
c) No. 14
d) No. 15

ANSWER KEY – COACH CHARLEY PELL (1979-1984)

171. A – Alabama.

172. B – 33 wins, 26 losses and 3 ties.

173. A – USC.

174. D – 1983. The Gators were 9-2-1 during the 1983 season. Coach Pell was replaced after the third game of the 1984 season when the team had one win, one loss and one tie.

175. A – No. 6. It came in the final 1983 AP Poll after the Gators finished at 9-2-1.

COACH GALEN HALL (1984-1989) & COACH GARY DARNELL (1989)

Question 176: After the third game of the season in 1984, Offensive Coordinator Galen Hall became Head Coach (and he remained in that position until the middle of the 1989 season when Coach Gary Darnell became the interim Head Coach). When Coach Hall took over (the fourth game of the 1984 season) the Gators were 1-1-1, how many consecutive games did the Gators win during the 1984 season after Coach Hall took over the head coaching duties?

a) 5 consecutive games
b) 6 consecutive games
c) 7 consecutive games
d) 8 consecutive games

Question 177: What was Coach Hall's career won-loss record at Florida as Head Coach, including postseason games?

a) 20-38-1
b) 30-28-1
c) 40-18-1
d) 50-8-1

Question 178: During this season the Gators had their best season record under Coach Hall. The Gators also had the best SEC record of 5-1 but the SEC Conference title was again taken away because of rule violations. The Gators finished with an overall record of 9-1-1.

a) 1985
b) 1986
c) 1987
d) 1988

Question 179: Coach Gary Darnell became the interim Head Coach in the middle of the 1989 season. What was the combined record of Coach Hall and Coach Darnell's?

a) 53-11-1
b) 43-22-1
c) 33-32-1
d) 23-42-1

Question 180: Beginning with Coach Hall's first full season in 1985 and continuing through the interim stint of Head Coach Darnell, what was the highest season-ending national AP ranking achieved by the Gators?

a) No. 5
b) No. 7
c) No. 9
d) No. 11

ANSWER KEY – COACH GALEN HALL (1984-1989) & COACH GARY DARNELL (1989)

176. D – 8 consecutive games. After the resignation of Coach Charley Pell, the Gators went undefeated the rest of the season to finish at 9-1-1. The Gators were undefeated in the conference (one tie) but the Gators first-ever SEC title was later taken away because of rule violations by the previous coach.

177. C – 40-18-1.

178. A – 1985.

179. B – 43-22-1.

180. A – No. 5. It came in 1985.

COACH STEVE SPURRIER (1990-2001)

Question 181: Steve Spurrier brought Florida football to its highest levels. He was not only an incredible player in the 1960s, but he was also an incredible Head Coach of the Gators. When was the first year that Steve Spurrier was a coach at the University of Florida?

a) 1978
b) 1989
c) 1990
d) 1996

Question 182: How many seasons was Coach Spurrier the Coach of the Year in the SEC?

a) 1
b) 3
c) 5
d) 7

Question 183: How many SEC Championships did the Gators win during Coach Spurrier's 12-year career as Head Coach at Florida?

a) 3
b) 4
c) 5
d) 6

Question 184: What was Coach Spurrier's 12-year won-loss record at Florida?

a) 122 wins, 27 losses and 1 tie
b) 112 wins, 37 losses and 1 tie
c) 102 wins, 47 losses and 1 tie
d) 92 wins, 57 losses and 1 tie

Question 185: During Coach Spurrier's tenure as the Gators Head Coach, how many times did the Gators appear in a bowl game?

a) 8
b) 9
c) 10
d) 11

ANSWER KEY – COACH STEVE SPURRIER (1990-2001)

181. A – 1978. You were probably thinking 1990, but in 1978 Coach Spurrier was the quarterbacks coach for Coach Doug Dickey. In 1989 he was the Head Coach at Duke University which won the ACC Championship. Coach Spurrier came home to the Gators as Head Coach in 1990. In 1996 he led the Gators to their first National Championship.

182. C – 5 times. He was SEC Coach of the Year in 1990, 1991, 1994, 1995 and 1996.

183. D – 6. He won SEC Championships in 1991, 1993, 1994, 1995, 1996 and 2000.

184. A – 122 wins, 27 losses and 1 tie. Note: Coach Spurrier is the only coach in major college history to win as many as 120 games in his first 12 seasons at one school!

185. D – 11 bowl games. Florida was one of only five schools to do so during that time period.

COACH RON ZOOK (2002-2004) & COACH CHARLIE STRONG (2004)

Question 186: Coach Ron Zook was named the Head Coach after Coach Spurrier departed following the 2001 season. Coach Zook had served as a Gator coach under Coach Spurrier in various capacities. In three seasons as Head Coach, what was Coach Zook's won-loss record?

a) 23-14
b) 13-24
c) 16-21
d) 21-16

Question 187: How many bowl games did Coach Zook lead the Gators to?

a) None
b) One
c) Two
d) Three

Question 188: Two of Coach Ron Zook's biggest wins came against this big SEC rival when the opponent was ranked No. 5 in 2002 and No. 4 in 2003.

a) Auburn University
b) Louisiana State University
c) University of Georgia
d) Vanderbilt University

Question 189: Coach Zook's final game coaching the Gators was a huge win, 20-13 against this big rival on the road. The Gators were unranked and their opponent was ranked No. 10. Coach Spurrier had not been able to defeat this team on the road. Which rival did Coach Zook defeat in his final game?

a) Louisiana State University
b) University of Tennessee
c) Florida State University
d) University of Alabama

Question 190: Coach Zook was praised by this coach for his recruiting skills following the Gators win in the 2006 BCS Championship Game because the many seniors on the team were recruited by Coach Zook and his staff.

a) Coach Galen Hall
b) Coach Ray Graves
c) Coach Steve Spurrier
d) Coach Urban Meyer

ANSWER KEY – COACH RON ZOOK (2002-2004) & COACH CHARLIE STRONG (2004)

186. A – 23-14.

187. C – Three. Coach Zook did not, however, coach the third bowl game. Coach Charlie Strong was named interim Head Coach for the Peach Bowl played on Dec. 31, 2004. The other bowl games were the Outback Bowl on Jan.1, 2003 and the Outback Bowl on Jan. 1, 2004. All three games were losses.

188. C – University of Georgia. The Gators whipped the Bulldogs 20-13 and 16-13 respectively, in 2002 and 2003.

189. C – Florida State University.

190. D – Coach Urban Meyer. It was reported that 22 of 24 starters in the game were recruited by Coach Zook and his staff.

COACH URBAN MEYER (2005-PRESENT)

Question 191: Including the 2009 season, Coach Urban Meyer has now completed five seasons as Head Coach of the Florida Gators. His Gator teams have accumulated numerous team and individual accomplishments. What years have the Gators won National Championships under the leadership of Coach Urban Meyer?

a) 2005, 2006
b) 2006, 2007
c) 2004, 2006
d) 2006, 2008

Question 192: What is Coach Urban Meyer's record during the first five seasons of his tenure at the University of Florida?

a) 57 wins, 10 losses
b) 56 wins, 11 losses
c) 54 wins, 13 losses
d) 52 wins, 15 losses

Question 193: The "traditional" foes of the Gators are Tennessee, Georgia and Florida State. What is the won-loss record of Coach Meyer against these teams as Gator Head Coach (through the 2009 season)?

a) 14 wins, 1 loss
b) 13 wins, 2 losses
c) 12 wins, 3 losses
d) 11 wins, 4 losses

Question 194: What position did Coach Meyer play in college?

a) Quarterback
b) End
c) Running Back
d) Defensive Back

Question 195: In 2004 (prior to coming to Florida) Coach Meyer was recognized as the National Coach of the Year. His undefeated team finished No. 4 in the nation. What is the name of the university?

a) Utah
b) Cincinnati
c) Bowling Green
d) Boise State

ANSWER KEY – COACH URBAN MEYER (2005-PRESENT)

191. D – in 2006 and 2008 the Gators won National Championships under the leadership of Coach Meyer, and *Sporting News* selected Coach Meyer as the College Football Coach of the Decade in September of 2009.

192. A – 57 wins and 10 losses.

193. A – 14 wins and 1 loss in five seasons.

194. D – Defensive back for University of Cincinnati.

195. A – University of Utah.

MORE FACTS ABOUT GATOR COACHES (1950-PRESENT)

Question 196: What does Coach Ray Graves (1960-69) have in common with Heisman Trophy winners Steve Spurrier, Danny Wuerffel and Tim Tebow?

a) All four won a National Championship as a player
b) All four were college quarterbacks
c) All four had a father who was/is a minister
d) All four had a father who was/is a college coach

Question 197: All of the following former Gator Head Coaches played professional football except for one. Which one of the following did not play professional football?

a) Coach Steve Spurrier
b) Coach Ray Graves
c) Coach Doug Dickey
d) Coach Galen Hall

Question 198: Which Head Coach (since 1950) was drafted by the Atlanta Braves and played professional baseball in the minors before starting his coaching career?

a) Coach Ray Graves
b) Coach Galen Hall
c) Coach Ron Zook
d) Coach Urban Meyer

Question 199: This former Head Coach of the Gators was an all-state selection in three sports in high school – football, basketball and baseball. However, he only played football for the Gators. Who is this all-around performer?

a) Coach Bob Woodruff
b) Coach Steve Spurrier
c) Coach Galen Hall
d) Coach Ron Zook

Question 200: Coach Spurrier made a couple of requests after being named Head Coach at Florida. What were they?

a) Add additional seating in the south and north end zones
b) Add additional seating in the south end zone and club seats on the west side
c) Replace turf with grass and increase student seating
d) Replace turf with grass and "un-retire" his No. 11 jersey and All-American Scot Brantley's No. 55 jersey

ANSWER KEY – MORE FACTS ABOUT GATOR COACHES (1950-PRESENT)

196. C – Their fathers were ministers. Note: Coach Graves's father was a Methodist Minister, Coach Spurrier's father was a Presbyterian Minister, Danny Wuerffel's father was an Air Force Chaplain and Tim Tebow's father is a missionary.

197. C – Coach Doug Dickey. Note: Coach Steve Spurrier played in the NFL from 1967-76. Coach Graves played in the NFL from 1942-46. And, Coach Galen Hall played from 1962-63.

198. D – Coach Urban Meyer.

199. B – Coach Steve Spurrier.

200. D – At Coach Spurrier's request, the turf was replaced with grass and his No. 11 jersey and the No. 55 jersey of All-American Scot Brantley were both "un-retired." As a replacement for the retirement of jerseys, the Ring of Honor was established.

5 JERSEY NUMBERS AND WALK-ONS

Most kids have a favorite player when growing up. The player may not have been the best player on the team, but that was okay. The kid usually "adopted" the jersey number of the player and the number became the favorite of the kid. Depending upon your age, one of the following numbers may have been your favorite during the years. Who wore the following jersey numbers in the year indicated? If you get 50 percent of these questions right you'll be doing very, very good – especially since multiple choice is not an option for most of the questions in this chapter!

JERSEY NUMBERS
(FIRST SET OF SIX – THE EASIEST!)

Question 201: Who wore…? Jersey No. 1, 2007-08, running back, All-Purpose, 1st Team American Football Coaches Association (AFCA) All-American 2008 and 1st Team All-American Rivals.com, 1st Team All-SEC (All-Purpose player). (Wore jersey No. 8 in 2006.) He now plays for the Minnesota Vikings.

Question 202: Who wore…? Jersey No. 7, 1993-96, quarterback, Heisman Trophy 1996, All-American 1st Team AP 1996. All-SEC 1st Team.

Question 203: Who wore…? Jersey No. 11, 1964-66, quarterback, Heisman Trophy 1966, All-American 1st Team AP 1996.

Question 204: Who wore…? Jersey No. 12, 2003-06, First Team quarterback of the 2006 National Champions.

Question 205: Who wore…? Jersey No. 15, 2006-09, quarterback, Heisman Trophy 2007, All-American AP 1st Team 2008, 1st Team All-SEC Coaches Team 2009, Heisman Trophy finalist 2008 and 2009, winner of the 2009 William V. Campbell Trophy (formerly known as the Draddy Trophy – given to the nation's top scholar-athlete).

ANSWER KEY – JERSEY NUMBERS (FIRST SET OF SIX – THE EASIEST!)

201. Percy Harvin – No. 1.

202. Danny Wuerffel – No. 7.

203. Steve Spurrier – No. 11.

204. Chris Leak – No. 12.

205. Tim Tebow – No. 15.

JERSEY NUMBERS
(SECOND SET OF SIX – SLIGHTLY MORE DIFFICULT!)

Question 206: Who wore…? Jersey No. 4, 1993-96, strong safety, All-American 3rd Team Football News 1995, 1st Team All-SEC.

Question 207: Who wore…? Jersey No. 18, 1985-88, free safety, All-American 1st Team AP 1988, Fergie Ferguson Award, 1st Team All-SEC. First-round pick of the Miami Dolphins.

Question 208: Who wore…? Jersey No. 19, 1994-96, wide receiver, All-American 1st Team American Football Coaches Association. (AFCA) 1996, 1st Team All-SEC. First-round pick of the New York Giants.

Question 209: Who wore…? Jersey No. 21, 1994-97, running back, All-American 1st Team Walter Camp 1997, 1st Team All-SEC. Played several years for the Jaguars in the NFL (a first-round pick).

Question 210: Who wore…? Jersey No. 21, 1977-80, wide receiver, All-American 1st Team Newspaper Enterprises Association (NEA). Played several years for the Cincinnati Bengals (second-round pick).

ANSWER KEY – JERSEY NUMBERS (SECOND SET OF SIX – SLIGHTLY MORE DIFFICULT!)

206. Lawrence Wright – No. 4.

207. Louis Oliver – No. 18.

208. Ike Hilliard – No. 19.

209. Fred Taylor – No. 21.

210. Cris Collinsworth – No. 21.

JERSEY NUMBERS (THIRD SET OF SIX – GETTING HARDER!)

Question 211: Who wore…? Jersey No. 22, 1987-89, running back, All-American 1st Team AP 1989, 1st Team All-SEC. He was a first-round pick of the Dallas Cowboys.

Question 212: Who wore…? Jersey No. 27, 1982-85, running back, Fergie Ferguson Award, 1st Team All-SEC. He was a first-round draft choice of the Chicago Bears.

Question 213: Who wore…? Jersey No. 33, 1990-93, running back, All-American 1st Team Football News 1993, 1st Team All-SEC. He was a second-round choice of the Tampa Bay Buccaneers.

Question 214: Who wore…? Jersey No. 45, 1969-71, wide receiver, All-American 1st Team United Press International (UPI) 1969. He was drafted by the Dallas Cowboys.

Question 215: Who wore…? Jersey No. 75, 1981-84, offensive tackle, All-American 1st Team AP 1984, 1st Team All-SEC. He was a first-round selection of the Detroit Lions.

ANSWER KEY – JERSEY NUMBERS (THIRD SET OF SIX – GETTING HARDER!)

211. Emmitt Smith – No. 22.

212. Neal Anderson – No. 27.

213. Errict Rhett – No. 33.

214. Carlos Alvarez - No. 45.

215. Lomas Brown – No. 75.

JERSEY NUMBERS
(FOURTH SET OF SIX – NOW IT'S GETTING TOUGH!)

Question 216: Who wore…? Jersey No. 22, 1968-69, defensive back, All-American 1st Team Football News. He played for the New York Jets.

Question 217: Who wore…? Jersey No. 33, 1966-68, fullback, All-American 1st Team Sporting News 1968, 1st Team All-SEC. He was a first-round selection of the LA Rams.

Question 218: Who wore…? Jersey No. 72, 1963-65, offensive guard, All-American 1st team National Broadcasting (NBC), 1st Team All-SEC. His jersey was No. 82 in 1963. Played professional football for the Pittsburgh Steelers and the Kansas City Chiefs.

Question 219: Who wore…? Jersey No. 88, 1980-83, linebacker, All-American 1st Team AP 1983, 1st Team All-SEC. He was a first-round pick of the Chicago Bears.

Question 220: Who wore…? Jersey No. 89, 1974-77, wide receiver, All-American 1st Team UPI 1977, 1st Team All-SEC, Fergie Ferguson Award. He was a first-round draft choice of the New Orleans Saints.

ANSWER KEY – JERSEY NUMBERS (FOURTH SET OF SIX – NOW IT'S GETTING TOUGH!)

216. Steve Tannen – 22.

217. Larry Smith – No. 33.

218. Larry Gagner – No. 72.

219. Wilber Marshall – 88.

220. Wes Chandler – No. 89.

JERSEY NUMBERS (FIFTH SET OF SIX – GETTING THREE RIGHT IS VERY GOOD!)

Question 221: Who wore…? Jersey No. 14, 1960-62, highly regarded quarterback, 2nd Team All-SEC.

Question 222: Who wore…? Jersey No. 14, 1963-65, defensive back, All-American 1st Team UPI, 1st Team All-SEC.

Question 223: Who wore…? Jersey No. 33, 1960-62, a highly regarded running back, he scored the final TD against Georgia Tech in an 18-17 upset win for the Gators in 1960. All-SEC 3rd Team. He became an NFL coach.

Question 224: Who wore…? Jersey No. 35, fullback 1962-64, All-American 1st Team American Football Coaches Association (AFCA), 1st Team All-SEC UPI and AP, Fergie Ferguson Award.

Question 225: Who wore…? Jersey No. 74, 1968-70, defensive end, All-American 1st Team Football Writers Association of America (FWAA). Played in the NFL (Los Angeles Rams).

ANSWER KEY – JERSEY NUMBERS (FIFTH SET OF SIX – GETTING THREE RIGHT IS VERY GOOD!)

221. Larry Libertore – No. 14.

222. Bruce Bennett – No. 14.

223. Lindy Infante – No. 33.

224. Larry Dupree – No. 35.

225. Jack Youngblood – No. 74.

JERSEY NUMBERS (SIXTH SET OF SIX – GETTING TWO RIGHT IS EXCELLENT!)

Admit it . . . you would have to be an old-timer to get these right!

Question 226: Who wore…? Jersey No. 11, 1950-51, an outstanding athlete who played both football and baseball. Ultimately became one of the owners of the Boston Red Sox.

Question 227: Who wore…? Jersey No. 20, 1951-53, fullback who continued his career in the pros with the Chicago Bears. He also played basketball for the Gators.

Question 228: Who wore…? Jersey No. 36, 1958-59, maybe the best punter in Gator history, averaged 44.9 yards per punt his senior year and punted for the Chicago Bears for 12 years. His 82-yard punt against Georgia is a Gator record.

Question 229: Who wore…? Jersey No. 67, 1953-56, offensive guard, All-American 1st Team Football Writers Association of America 1956, SEC Lineman of the Year (1956). Played in the Canadian Football League.

Question 230: Who wore…? Jersey No. 75, 1950-52, offensive/defensive lineman, All-American 1st Team AP 1952.

ANSWER KEY – JERSEY NUMBERS (SIXTH SET OF SIX – GETTING TWO RIGHT IS EXCELLENT!)

226. Haywood Sullivan – No. 11.

227. Rick Casares – No. 20.

228. Bobby Joe Green - No. 36.

229. John Barrow – No. 67.

230. Charley LaPradd – No. 75.

WALK-ONS, SOME FACTS AND FIGURES

Some of the very best athletes on the Gator football teams throughout the years have been walk-ons. They persevered practice sessions and waited for their opportunity to demonstrate what they could do on the field.

The Florida Gators are known for its walk-ons who have made significant contributions to its football program. Many walk-ons have earned scholarships and have been recognized for their athletic and/or academic achievements. Some walk-ons have even made it to the pros.

The following walk-ons really became "household names" because of their contributions to the Gator football team. At least 13 former Gator walk-ons who earned scholarships have continued their football careers in the pros.

Question 231: How many walk-on athletes have earned a football scholarship at the University of Florida since 1990?

a) 15
b) 25
c) 35
d) 45

Question 232: How many players on the 1985 team were originally walk-ons when they started at UF? The 1985 team finished fifth in the nation with a 9-1-1 record.

a) 16
b) 18
c) 20
d) 22

Question 233: How many players on the 1991 team (SEC Champs) were originally walk-ons?

a) 12
b) 16
c) 22
d) 26

Question 234: How many Gator walk-ons have earned Academic All-SEC honors (through 2008)?

a) 96
b) 106
c) 116
d) 126

Question 235: The BCS National Championship team of 2006 had how many walk-ons, including five athletes who earned scholarships?

a) 16
b) 20
c) 26
d) 36

ANSWER KEY – WALK-ONS, SOME FACTS AND FIGURES

231. D – 45 walk-on players.

232. B – 18 walk-on players.

233. D – 26 walk-on players.

234. C – 116 walk-on players.

235. D – 36 walk-on players.

WALK-ONS, PUNTERS & PLACE KICKERS WHO EARNED SCHOLARSHIPS

Question 236: This place kicker was the 1993 Lou Groza National Place Kicker of the Year. He booted 14 field goals and 65 PATs in 1994. He wore jersey No. 6 in 1993 and 1994 but wore jersey No. 43 in 1992. He was also a 2nd Team All-American choice.

Question 237: This punter played for the Gators in 1970-71 and wore jersey No. 6. He continued his career in the NFL. He received All-Pro honors in the NFL. He is now the director of Gator Boosters, Inc.

Question 238: This former walk-on set five NCAA place kicking records in five different categories as a Gator. He played 1982-84 and wore jersey No. 3.

Question 239: This place kicker earned 1st Team All-SEC honors and played during 1974-76. He wore jersey No. 3.

Question 240: This place kicker was a 2nd Team All-American choice in 1999 and was a two-time semifinalist for the Groza National Place Kicker of the Year Award. He wore jersey No. 49 and played for the Gators from 1998-2001.

ANSWER KEY – WALK-ONS, PUNTERS & PLACE KICKERS WHO EARNED SCHOLARSHIPS

236. Judd Davis, 1993-94.

237. John James, 1970-71.

238. Bobby Raymond, 1982-84.

239. David Posey, 1974-76.

240. Jeff Chandler, 1998-2001.

WALK-ONS, OFFENSIVE PLAYERS WHO EARNED SCHOLARSHIPS

Question 241: This former walk-on became the starting quarterback for the Gators and was selected as the SEC Player of the Year in 1984. He wore jersey No. 12 and played from 1984-87.

Question 242: Who was the receiver that completed his career in 1995 after scoring 31 touchdowns? He was an All-SEC selection and 2nd Team All-American. He wore jersey No. 28 and played from 1992-95.

Question 243: This long snapper earned a scholarship in 2006 and handled all the long snaps for the Gators through the 2008 National Championship season. He wore jersey No. 43. He was named as a finalist for the Draddy Trophy – often referred to as the "Academic Heisman." He played from 2005-08.

Question 244: A wide receiver, this walk-on was named Academic All-American and winner of the National Football Foundation Scholar Athlete Award in 1984. He played from 1982-84 and wore jersey No. 86.

Question 245: This Gator wore jersey No. 91, and was a tight end from 1994-96. He continued his football career with the Chicago Bears.

ANSWER KEY – WALK-ONS, OFFENSIVE PLAYERS WHO EARNED SCHOLARSHIPS

241. Kerwin Bell, quarterback, 1984-87.

242. Chris Doering, wide receiver, 1992-95.

243. James Smith, long snapper, 2005-08.

244. Gary Rolle, wide receiver, 1982-84.

245. Tremayne Allen, tight end, 1994-96.

WALK-ONS, DEFENSIVE PLAYERS WHO EARNED SCHOLARSHIPS

Question 246: This defensive back was a winner of the Fergie Ferguson Award in 1988 and was selected in the first-round of the NFL draft in 1989. He was the first defensive back in Gator history to be a two-time All-American. He wore jersey No. 18. He played from 1985-88.

Question 247: This defensive back wore Jersey No. 20, 1961-63, and continued his career with the Buffalo Bills.

Question 248: This walk-on linebacker led the Gators in tackles in 1988 and 1989. He wore jersey No. 45.

Question 249: This defensive back was a 2nd Team All-SEC selection and continued his football career in the pros. He wore jersey No. 23, 1963-65.

Question 250: A defensive end that played from 1972-74, this walk-on earned a scholarship and was a 1st Team All-SEC UPI selection. He wore jersey No. 90. He was selected in the eighth-round of the 1975 NFL draft by the San Francisco 49ers.

ANSWER KEY – WALK-ONS, DEFENSIVE PLAYERS WHO EARNED SCHOLARSHIPS

246. Louis Oliver, defensive back, 1985-88.

247. Hagood Clark, defensive back, 1961-63.

248. Pat Moorer, linebacker, 1986-89.

249. Allen Trammell, defensive back, 1963-65.

250. Preston Kendrick, defensive end, 1972-74.

6 THE DEFENDING CHAMPS

Three years, two National Championships, one final goal: perfection. The Gators began 2009 ranked No. 1, and why not? After all, Florida beat Oklahoma in the BCS National Championship Game and in the days that followed learned the core of its defensive unit would be returning for another season. That's the entire unit, first and second team.

And that's without even mentioning Tim Tebow.

You do remember "The Promise" after Florida's 31-30 loss to Ole Miss on September 27, 2008? Tebow said: "You will never see any player in the entire country play harder than I will the rest of the season. And you will not see someone push the rest of the team as hard as I will push everybody for the rest of the season, and you will never see a team play harder than we will the rest of the season." He made good on his promise, too. His words inspired his team, its fans, and even his coaches. Florida ran the table and won the National Championship.

Ah, but it wasn't a perfect season.

And in his promise – those now legendary words that are immortalized outside The Swamp, where fans come and pause for a moment and reflect and give thanks – Tebow plainly stated his goal from the very beginning, Florida's goal, was perfection.

So . . . after winning the National Championship, when Tebow made his plans known, that he was returning for his senior year, there was little debate among the pollsters regarding which team would be the early favorite in 2009. Not that it mattered what the pollsters thought anyway, because Coach Meyer, Tebow, Brandon Spikes, and the rest of the defending National Championship squad had already made it clear what Florida's expectations would be – another SEC title, perhaps another Heisman, but more than anything, a shot at winning a third National Championship in four years.

In a word: *perfection.*

Florida's 2009 Senior Class will be remembered as one of the most successful in the history of NCAA football, and its heart and soul, Tim Tebow, will be remembered as one of the greatest collegiate players of all-time. The first five chapters of this book were dedicated to the history of Florida football – but here in Chapter Six it's all about the Gators pursuit of perfection in 2009. Here you will find a game-by-game recap of the 2009 season from the opener through the Sugar Bowl with highlights, quotes, and a blow-by-blow account of the Gators quest to repeat as National Champs – and of course, we test the level of your fandom one last time with a series of questions from every game.

The crowd is gathering outside The Swamp. It's time for the Gator Walk. Here we go. It's the final chapter.

Good luck!

CHARLESTON SOUTHERN

The AP labeled Florida "an overwhelming favorite to repeat as national champs" after the Gators swamped Charleston Southern 62-3 to open the 2009 season.

Urban Meyer offered a more tempered appraisal of his team's performance, saying, "It's hard to evaluate that game." The Gators were nearly flawless, true, but it wasn't against a top-tier opponent.

Key stats: Tim Tebow was 10 for 15 passing for 188 yards and accounted for two touchdowns, one rushing and one passing. Jeff Demps scored two rushing touchdowns, Chris Rainey broke a 76-yard rushing touchdown, and Brandon James returned a kickoff 85 yards for a score.

Now for some trivia:

Question 251: Brandon James said afterwards, "It feels good to go on and get it out the way the first game. Just to get it my senior year, the first game of the season, feels real good." What was he talking about? The kickoff return, of course, and for good reason – that's because it had been 123 games since the last time a Gator returned a kickoff for a touchdown. Bo Carroll did it on October 9, 1999, and James was determined to get one before he graduated. Up to this point, James was the best return man in the game *without* returning a kickoff for a touchdown. In fact, James *had* returned kickoffs for touchdowns on more than one occasion previously, but all of them were negated due to penalties. How many times previously had Brandon James returned a kickoff for a touchdown only to see it called back due to a penalty?

a) 2
b) 3
c) 4
d) 5

Question 252: Florida's win improved Coach Meyer's career record to 9-0 in season openers. It also extended a lengthy winning streak for Florida in season openers. With the victory over Charleston Southern, how many consecutive season openers has Florida won?

a) 16
b) 18
c) 20
d) 22

Question 253: Who scored Florida's first touchdown of the 2009 season? It came on an eight-yard play with 11:05 left in the opening quarter.

a) Jeff Demps
b) Chris Rainey
c) Tim Tebow
d) Aaron Hernandez

Question 254: Florida's defense forced one turnover in the game, an interception. Who got the first pick of the season for the Gators?

a) Brandon Spikes
b) Major Wright
c) Ahmad Black
d) Ryan Stamper

ANSWER KEY – CHARLESTON SOUTHERN

251. B – 3.

252. C – 20.

253. A – Jeff Demps.

254. B – Major Wright.

TROY

Week two unfolded exactly as planned, a 56-6 tune-up for Tennessee. Florida's offense actually started slow against Troy, but it was due more to the bad weather than it was the Trojans defense – and once the offense got going, nothing could stop it. The Gators ran off 28 unanswered points in the second quarter and led 35-3 at the half.

It was impressive, but no one at The Swamp – especially the players – mistook it for anything other than a warm-up for a grueling SEC schedule. Florida receiver David Nelson said it best afterwards, "The season starts now."

Key stats: Florida amassed 663 yards of total offense. In case you're not sure, *that's a lot*, even when you're playing a weaker opponent. Tim Tebow was 14 for 22 passing and he accounted for five touchdowns, four through the air and one on the ground. Riley Cooper caught five passes for 82 yards and a score. Cooper also brought fans to their feet with his *blocking*. He actually was hitting people so hard that his helmet flew off no less than four times during the game, prompting Coach Meyer to joke afterwards, "I guess I'm the helmet cop, too."

Now for some trivia:

Question 255: Tim Tebow scored on a four-yard run with 8:04 left in the half to give the Gators a 21-3 lead. It was the 45th rushing touchdown of his career, tying him for third all-time in the SEC. Who was previously alone in third place all-time with 45 rushing touchdowns in the SEC?

a) Dalton Hilliard
b) Herschel Walker
c) Carnell Williams
d) Kevin Faulk

Question 256: The easy win over Troy allowed the Gators to tie a school record for consecutive victories. After improving to 2-0 on the 2009 season, how many consecutive games had the Gators won to equal the school record?

a) 11
b) 12

c) 13
d) 14

Question 257: With 87 yards and a touchdown on only seven carries, who was the Gators leading rusher against Troy?

a) Jeff Demps
b) Chris Rainey
c) Tim Tebow
d) Brandon James

ANSWER KEY – TROY

255. C – Carnell Williams.

256. B – 12.

257. A – Jeff Demps.

TENNESSEE

Remember this? "I'm really looking forward to embracing some of the great traditions at the University of Tennessee, for instance the Vol Walk, running through the T, singing Rocky Top all night long after we beat Florida next year. It will be a blast."

That was Lane Kiffin, of course.

Kiffin stirred things up with his ambitious (and delusional) comments when he was introduced as the Vols new coach some nine months earlier, and the week leading up to the Tennessee game the media tried its best to instigate a war of words between the two schools. Coach Meyer wouldn't take the bait, however, saying, "There's a bunch of great athletes on both sides of the ball. The thing we'll never let happen around here is it's about a coach or coaches. And I told those players that. This is about preparation and playing a game. That's what it is. Period."

Coach Meyer might have downplayed the bulletin board material provided by Kiffin, but make no mistake about it, from the coaches to the players to every fan that makes up Gator Nation, this was a date to be circled on the calendar. When the date finally arrived, Florida was the heavy favorite – in fact, a 30-point win wouldn't have surprised anybody – but this is the SEC, and no matter the odds, beating a conference rival such as Tennessee should never be treated as a cakewalk.

And it wasn't.

Still, for Tennessee to pull the upset it was going to need some help – like injuries and illnesses on the Florida bench. And unfortunately three of Florida's key offensive players fell prey to just that. Deonte Thompson was out due to a hamstring injury, Jeff Demps played with a fever hovering around 101, and Aaron Hernandez was suffering from the flu.

Not that too many Gator fans were worried.

Not until, at least, the end of the first quarter, when the score was tied at a measly 3-3. Brandon James returned the opening kick 50 yards to the Tennessee 30, but Florida's offense managed only one first down and ten yards before stalling. Caleb Sturgis kicked a 37-yard field goal to put Florida on top, 3-0.

And then . . . frustration.

Tennessee put together a 15-play drive that covered 66 yards and took 8:33 off the clock. Florida's defense buckled down and stopped Tennessee at the seven, but a 24-yard field goal by Daniel Lincoln tied things up, 3-3.

Florida's second possession began with just 3:00 left in the first quarter. The Gators put together a nice drive that lasted 11 plays and covered 72 yards, and Tebow finished it off early in the second quarter with a rushing touchdown from one yard out. With that score, Tebow moved into a tie for second all-time in the SEC for rushing touchdowns, and Florida was up 10-3.

The Gators defense forced a quick punt and things were looking good. Florida had the ball back and was looking to extend its lead, but after starting at its own 20 a quick false start followed by Chris Rainey getting stuffed behind the line of scrimmage put the Gators in a second and long situation – and then it got worse. Tebow got picked off on second down, and just like that the Vols were set up in the red zone. Tennessee got a first down to set up a goal-to-go situation inside the Florida five, but the Gators defense held and another kick by Daniel Lincoln made it 10-6.

Florida took the ball 52 yards on 11 plays on its next possession, but stalled inside the Tennessee 15 and had to settle for another field goal just before half, and the Gators went into the locker room with a 13-6 lead.

Not exactly the way we drew it up.

A blowout was not in the works. It was defense that dominated the day, and in the end it was Florida's defense that won the game. The Gators scored ten unanswered points in the third quarter, and after giving up a fourth quarter touchdown, held on for a 23-13 victory. Tim Tebow said afterwards, "It wasn't how we envisioned or hoped, but it's a win and it's good enough for all of us."

Key stats: Two streaks ended but one very important streak was kept alive. Tim Tebow's streak of games with at least one passing touchdown and Florida's streak of scoring at least 30 points against SEC opponents both came to an end – the Gators winning streak, however, continued, setting a new school record. Urban Meyer improved to 5-0 vs. Tennessee since taking to the Gators sideline.

Now for some trivia:

Question 258: Tebow's streak of games with a passing touchdown, the longest in the nation, came to an end. How many consecutive games had Tebow thrown at least one touchdown pass?

a) 26
b) 28
c) 30
d) 32

Question 259: It was the ninth time in Tennessee history that the Volunteers played against a team ranked No. 1 in the nation, and Coach Kiffin, his players, and Tennessee fans everywhere were hoping to knock the Gators out of the top spot. Thankfully it didn't work out – but just how many times *have* the Volunteers actually knocked off the nation's No. 1 ranked team?

a) 0
b) 1
c) 2
d) 3

Question 260: Tennessee quarterback Jonathan Crompton said afterwards, "I'm not happy." And there was no reason he should be. Florida's defense held him to 11 for 19 passing for 93 yards, no touchdowns, and two picks. Which two Florida defenders intercepted a Crompton pass?

a) Joe Haden and Ahmad Black
b) Ahmad Black and Brandon Spikes
c) Brandon Spikes and Joe Haden
d) Carlos Dunlap and Major Wright

Question 261: Florida's defense *was* stingy. How many total yards did Tennessee's offense manage against the Gators defense?

a) 190
b) 200
c) 210
d) 220

Question 262: Who was Florida's leading rusher with 76 yards on 24 carries?

a) Jeff Demps
b) Tim Tebow
c) Chris Rainey
d) Emmanuel Moody

ANSWER KEY – TENNESSEE

258. C – 30.

259. C – 2.

260. A – Joe Haden and Ahmad Black.

261. C – 210.

262. B – Tim Tebow.

KENTUCKY

Tennessee defensive coordinator Monte Kiffin apparently didn't "find the blueprint" to stopping the Gators offensive attack – give the Tennessee defense and its coach some credit, of course, but it turns out the flu was running rampant in the Gator locker room and in the days leading up to Florida's next SEC showdown it was so bad that a separate plane carried several players – including Tim Tebow – to Lexington. There was even speculation that Tebow might not play.

Well, so much for that.

It was 31-0 at the end of the first quarter. Kentucky Coach Rich Brooks later said, "We got our fannies kicked all over the field in every phase."

No kidding.

It was a great game for the Gators . . . right up until the moment in the third quarter when Tebow was sacked by Taylor Wyndham. On his way down, Tebow's head viciously struck teammate Marcus Gilbert's leg. And then the crowd went silent and Gator Nation held its collective breath as Tebow lay motionless on the ground.

Tebow was taken by ambulance to the hospital where he spent the night with concussion-like symptoms. Coach Meyer said, "I don't know, I think it's a concussion. I think he'll be all right. He took a pretty good shot." Florida was leading 31-7 and had no problem finishing the game, winning by a final of 41-7. Of course the final score was the last thing on everyone's mind. Coach Meyer added, "He asked me 'Did I hold onto the ball?' I told him he did and he winked at me and said 'It's great to be a Gator.'"

Key stats: Tebow was 5 for 10 passing, good for 103 yards and a touchdown. He also rushed 16 times for 123 yards and two scores, and moved into sole possession of second place on the SEC all-time rushing touchdowns list. Kentucky was just 3 for 16 on third down conversions and totaled just 179 yards of offense for the entire game.

Now for some trivia:

Question 263: Florida's defense and special teams continued to come up with big plays, including two more interceptions – one each for Janoris Jenkins and Major Wright, who gave Kentucky quarterback Mike Hartline fits all day. Florida also scored a special teams touchdown off a blocked punt in the first quarter to go up 17-0. Who blocked the punt and scored the touchdown?

a) Carlos Dunlap
b) Brandon Spikes
c) Chris Rainey
d) Brandon Hicks

Question 264: Florida's offensive outburst in the first quarter was quite impressive – four touchdowns and a field goal in the opening 15 minutes of play. Who caught a 44-yard pass from Tim Tebow on the final play of the first quarter to give Florida its fourth touchdown of the game?

a) Riley Cooper
b) Aaron Hernandez
c) David Nelson
d) Jeff Demps

Question 265: Kentucky managed just 86 of its 179 total yards on the ground while Florida had five different players rush for at least 30 yards each: Tim Tebow, Jeff Demps, Emmanuel Moody, Mike Gillislee, and Chris Rainey. How many total yards did the Gators amass on the ground vs. Kentucky?

a) 342
b) 352
c) 362
d) 372

Question 266: Florida has made quite a habit out of beating Kentucky. In addition to extending its record winning streak and the longest winning streak in the nation, the Gators also extended the nation's second longest active winning streak by one team vs. another. It was the 11th consecutive victory for the Gators in Lexington. How many consecutive times have the Gators beaten the Wildcats overall?

a) 21
b) 22
c) 23
d) 24

ANSWER KEY – KENTUCKY

263. C – Chris Rainey.

264. B – Aaron Hernandez.

265. C – 362.

266. C – 23.

LSU

When your team leader and Heisman-winning quarterback suffers a concussion and your next contest is on the road in Baton Rouge . . . well, let's just say the Gators were especially grateful this season's bye week came at the perfect time.

Tebow got two weeks off to recover before facing LSU. And in that time the media descended upon Gainesville, as did a concussion specialist from Pittsburgh. Gator Nation waited for updates, information, indicators, anything at all that would hint one way or another whether or not Tebow was recovering, whether or not he would be ready for the crucial showdown on the road in Baton Rouge, and worst case scenario, whether or not the concussion threatened the rest of his senior season.

Coach Meyer said, "It was a tough deal and I kept saying, 'Would I play my son?'" He added, "You know Tim. It was 'Let me play. Let me play.' Nonstop."

And when the word finally came – yes, Tebow is going to play – two weeks of collectively holding our breath's turned into a huge sigh of relief. As for the game itself, it was huge: No. 1 vs. No. 4, a road game for Florida in one of the toughest venues for visiting teams to play in the SEC, and National Championship implications hanging in the balance.

There were 93,129 screaming fans in a hostile environment and Florida's quarterback offered this assessment: "This place is one of my favorite stadiums to play in. It just gets your adrenaline going." As if Tebow ever needs something to pump up his adrenaline. Anyway, there was quite a change in the crowd's behavior from the opening kickoff until the final minutes of the fourth quarter – it was really loud, and then it was really quiet.

It was loud when LSU started the game's first possession at its own 25. Six plays later the Gators stellar defense forced a punt. The Tigers managed eight possessions in the game and to say they were dominated by the Gators defense is an understatement. In order of possession, here's what LSU did on offense: six plays, punt; five plays, punt; 12 plays, field goal; three plays, interception; three plays, punt; five plays, punt; four plays, turnover on downs; ten plays, turnover on downs. LSU's offense held the ball for only 3:15 during the fourth quarter, during which time it ran 14 plays but gained only 37 yards.

LSU quarterback Jordan Jefferson was sacked five times. The Tigers were held to just 162 total yards on offense, and only 66 on the ground. LSU was just 1 for 9 on third down conversions.

As for the Gators offense, well, thanks to the stellar play of the defense, Tebow & Co. did enough to get the win, 13-3.

It might have been the loudest crowd the Gators have ever faced when the offense began its first drive of the game backed up inside their own ten. After a false start penalty, Florida faced a second and 11 from its own six-yard line, and was forced to use a timeout.

And yeah, the crowd *loved* it.

It got a little quieter, however, when Aaron Hernandez picked up 16 yards and a first down. Two plays later Jeff Demps rushed for 25 yards. The next play went to Hernandez for eight yards and suddenly Florida was almost in field goal range.

And the crowd? Still loud, but not loving it nearly so much. Florida's opening drive ran 13 plays, 82 yards, and took 8:11 off the clock before stalling at the LSU 11-yard line. Caleb Sturgis put it through the uprights and Florida was on top, 3-0.

In the second quarter the crowd got back into the game in a big way when LSU drove 77 yards on 12 plays. The Gator defense held on three successive goal-to-go plays, however, and the Tigers stalled at the Florida two-yard line, but tied the game 3-3. That was huge, because after the ensuing kickoff Tebow drove the Gators 80 yards on eight plays, the last a 24-yard touchdown strike to Riley Cooper.

And that was enough.

Sturgis added a fourth quarter field goal to make the final 13-3, but Florida's defense *dominated* the game. LSU never sniffed the end zone in the second half. LSU's leading receiver was Brandon LaFell, who caught four passes for 44 yards and said after the game, "Those guys have a pretty good defense."

You think?

Key stats: Time of possession heavily favored Florida – 36:30 to 23:30. Tebow was 11 for 16, good for 134 yards and a touchdown. LSU's quarterback Jordan Jefferson was 11 for 17, good for 96 yards – but no score. Both quarterbacks got picked once – the big difference maker though? Florida's ground attack – the Gators tallied

193 yards on the ground, nearly three times as much as the 66 yards for the Tigers.

Now for some trivia:

Question 267: It's always tough to win conference games when you play in the SEC, especially on the road – and coming into the FL vs. LSU matchup, a good number of pundits gave the nod to LSU because the Tigers were riding a pretty remarkable streak. And what was that streak? Consecutive wins during night games at Tiger Stadium. The question then . . . how many consecutive night games had LSU won at Tiger Stadium?

a) 20
b) 22
c) 24
d) 26

Question 268: It was the seventh time Coach Meyer had been on the sidelines for the Gators following a bye week. With the victory, what did Coach Meyer's record improve to following bye weeks?

a) 7-0
b) 6-1
c) 5-2
d) 4-3

Question 269: The rushing game combined with such strong defensive play allowed the Gators to control the clock and time of possession. Who led the ground attack for the Gators with 86 yards on 16 carries?

a) Tim Tebow
b) Emmanuel Moody
c) Jeff Demps
d) Chris Rainey

Question 270: The Gators sacked LSU quarterback Jordan Jefferson five times. Who was responsible for 2.5 of those sacks?

a) Brandon Spikes
b) Carlos Dunlap

c) Brandon Hicks
d) Dustin Doe

Question 271: Tim Tebow said, "On offense, we didn't' execute the best but we played really hard." The Gators won 13-3, but that was the lowest winning point total for Florida since Urban Meyer took over as Head Coach in 2005. In his first season, Coach Meyer led the Gators to a 14-10 victory against . . . which SEC opponent?

a) LSU
b) Tennessee
c) Georgia
d) South Carolina

Question 272: Florida's defense snapped LSU's winning streak during night games at Tiger Stadium, and in the process it continued a very impressive streak of its own. Florida picked off a pass for the 17th consecutive game. Which Gator defender kept the interception streak alive?

a) Carlos Dunlap
b) Joe Haden
c) Brandon Spikes
d) Major Wright

ANSWER KEY – LSU

267. B – 22.

268. A – 7-0.

269. C – Jeff Demps.

270. A – Brandon Spikes.

271. C – Georgia.

272. B – Joe Haden.

ARKANSAS

Florida returned home to take on Arkansas. The Razorbacks came into the game only 3-2, but were riding high off consecutive thrashings of Texas A&M (47-19) and No. 17 Auburn (44-23). And it's worth repeating, there's no such thing as an easy game in the SEC – just ask Caleb Sturgis, who kicked a 27-yard field goal with nine ticks left on the clock to give Florida a 23-20 victory. Or ask Tim Tebow, who after leading the Gators 69 yards down the field to set up the winning kick closed his eyes, unable to watch.

Arkansas shut Florida's offense down in the first half and carried a 10-3 lead into the break.

The last time the Gators had lost, remember, was vs. Ole Miss, which led to Tebow's impromptu speech, now better known as The Promise. It felt an awful lot like the Ole Miss game as Florida's struggles continued in the second half.

On the day, Tebow was sacked six times, Florida lost four fumbles, dropped three passes, missed a field goal, was only 4 for 13 on third down conversions, and scored only once during its first four trips into the red zone. Coach Meyer reflected, "You usually don't win that kind of game."

With the scored tied 20-20, it all came down to one final drive. Tebow said, "I always knew we had a shot. We were just going to keep believing until the last second." It was getting hard to believe after Florida's first five possessions: missed field goal, punt, fumble, fumble, and fumble. After Florida tied the game in the fourth, Arkansas had a chance to go back on top with 3:08 to play, but the Razorbacks missed a 38-yard field goal attempt. And then Florida took over on offense. The ensuing drive covered 69 yards on 14 plays and took 2:59 off the clock. Tebow passed for 30 yards and ran for 22 on the final drive – and Riley Cooper caught a crucial third down pass on one knee after he'd fallen down – to set Sturgis up for the game-winner.

And Tebow couldn't watch.

Ole Miss was probably on his mind throughout the second half, couldn't blame him if it was. And when Sturgis was good from 27 yards out? "Once I heard everybody cheering and opened my eyes and saw we made the field goal, that was fun," Tebow said.

Key stats: Caleb Sturgis also kicked a 51-yard field goal in the third quarter and was 3 for 4 on the day. The game's outcome could have been much different if not for the kicking of both teams. Alex Tejada was 2 for 4 on the day for Arkansas.

Now for some trivia:

Question 273: It was a big win, as it kept Florida's perfect season alive – but it was also a big win personally for Coach Meyer. It was his 50th career win in the SEC, and he did it in record fashion – tying Frank Thomas (Alabama) as the fastest coach in SEC history to reach 50 wins. How many games did it take Frank Thomas and Urban Meyer to reach 50 wins?

a) 57
b) 59
c) 61
d) 63

Question 274: It was a record day for Tim Tebow too. Despite losing two fumbles and getting sacked six times, Tebow became the all-time leader in SEC history for career touchdowns (combined rushing and passing). Tebow's third quarter touchdown pass gave him 123 combined rushing and passing touchdowns in his career. Who did Tebow surpass in the record book and relegate to second place all-time?

a) Peyton Manning
b) Eli Manning
c) Danny Wuerffel
d) Pat Sullivan

Question 275: Not only did Tebow's touchdown pass earn him a spot in the SEC record book, but at the time it was also the longest touchdown pass of his career. Who caught the 77-yard touchdown pass that put Tim Tebow in the record book for combined rushing and passing touchdowns?

a) Riley Cooper
b) Aaron Hernandez
c) Deonte Thompson
d) Brandon James

Question 276: It was the ninth meeting between Florida and Arkansas. What did the Gators record improve to all-time vs. the Razorbacks?

a) 9-0
b) 8-1
c) 7-2
d) 6-3

ANSWER KEY – ARKANSAS

273. B – 59.

274. C – Danny Wuerffel.

275. C – Deonte Thompson.

276. B – 8-1.

MISSISSIPPI STATE

After escaping Arkansas, it was back on the road for another conference game, this time at Mississippi State to visit an old friend – former offensive coordinator Dan Mullen, now the Bulldogs Head Coach.

All-American linebacker Brandon Spikes, who suffered a groin injury vs. Arkansas, was just one of several key Gators forced to watch from the sideline. Taking into account Coach Mullen's intimate knowledge of the Gators offense, Florida's injuries, and the close scores vs. LSU and Arkansas, there were many who thought Florida's date in Starkville had upset written all over it. If they'd known Tim Tebow would throw two interceptions – both returned for TDs – they'd have been *sure* of it.

And of course, they'd have been *wrong*.

Florida won 29-19, thanks to another strong defensive effort. Coach Meyer said afterwards, "As an offense, we're not well right now." Adding, "Tim's not trying to be a hero, but we might be asking him to do too much." Tebow had nothing to say afterwards, quickly boarding the team bus without answering any questions from the media.

As for the scoring, it was Tebow who put the Gators in front with a 26-yard run in the second quarter, breaking a 3-3 tie. Florida led 13-3 in the final seconds of the first half when freshman Johnthan Banks picked off a Tebow pass and returned it 100 yards for a touchdown. Florida was looking at a potential 20-3 lead at the half, but instead it was 13-10.

Both teams traded field goals in the third quarter, and Florida clung to a three-point lead in the fourth until Chris Rainey ran one in from eight yards out to put the Gators up 22-13. The PAT failed. And if the Gators offense struggled to put the Bulldogs away, the Gators defense was more than up for the task. Less than a minute after Rainey's score, Dustin Doe returned a pick 23 yards to make it 29-13 (this being the play in which Doe allegedly stepped out of bounds *and* fumbled before crossing the goal line, although the score held up under review). On State's next possession, it was Major Wright who picked off Tyson Lee with 4:01 left on the clock, seemingly ending any hope for an upset for the home team.

And then Johnthan Banks struck again.

The freshman (and yes he really spells his name that way) picked off another Tebow pass, and returned this one for a touchdown as well – this time from 20 yards out – to make it 29-19. The two-point conversion failed and Florida escaped Starkville with its perfect season still intact.

Key stats: Tebow's rushing touchdown was the 49th of his career, tying him with Herschel Walker for the most in SEC history. Florida's offense might have "struggled" but it still totaled 249 yards on the ground, compared to the 237 *total* yards Mississippi State managed against the Gators tough defense. The Gators defense also picked off three passes.

Now for some trivia:

Question 277: Florida's best-in-the-nation winning streak continued, reaching 17 games. The Gators also snapped a losing streak in Starkville. How many consecutive road games had the Gators lost to Mississippi State in Starkville?

a) 3
b) 4
c) 5
d) 6

Question 278: Florida also improved to 7-0 for the first time in quite a while. When was the last season that the Gators started 7-0?

a) 1985
b) 1991
c) 1995
d) 1996

Question 279: Tim Tebow rushed for 88 yards on 22 carries, but he was *not* the Gators leading rusher. Who did lead the Gators vs. Mississippi State with 90 yards on 12 carries?

a) Jeff Demps
b) Chris Rainey
c) Emmanuel Moody
d) Brandon James

ANSWER KEY – MISSISSIPPI STATE

277. B – 4.

278. D – 1996.

279. B – Chris Rainey.

GEORGIA

Florida took out a month's worth of frustration on Georgia in The World's Largest Outdoor Cocktail Party, 41-17.

Georgia showed up with a different look in terms of apparel (no silver pants, no red helmets) but on the field it was pretty much a repeat of Florida's dominant 49-10 performance from 2008. "New helmets and black paints ain't going to make you win the game," said Ryan Stamper.

Now that's a good line.

And there were plenty of words being said back and forth between these two rivals, especially after Georgia's excessive celebration in 2007 that motivated Florida in 2008, and then Coach Meyer's two timeouts in the final 44 seconds of the Gators 2008 blowout . . . timeouts that were supposed to motivate Georgia in 2009, after all, the Georgia coaching staff plastered pictures of Coach Meyer calling for those timeouts all over their workout facility in the days leading up to the game.

Well, it didn't work.

Tim Tebow put the Gators out in front early with two TD passes in the first quarter. Georgia came back though with ten straight points in the second quarter to seemingly make a game of it – and after the TD that made it 14-10 Georgia celebrated in a manner very similar to the excessive celebration bit back in 2007. Cue Stamper again: "That's a bunch of fake juice, coaches trying to get their players going because it was a pretty close game."

Fake juice. Now that's a *great* line!

And unlike Georgia, Stamper did more than just talk – his outstanding defensive performance included an interception.

Florida's offense then ran off ten straight of its own to take a 24-10 lead into the half. After trading touchdowns in the third quarter, Florida tacked on ten more in the fourth for the 41-17 final.

It was the first time in a month of SEC play that Florida was clicking in all aspects of the game, and once more, according to Stamper, "If we play all phases of the game we're a very hard team to beat and we have every right to be the No. 1 team in the country.

Key stats: Tim Tebow was 15 for 21 passing, good for 164 yards and two touchdowns. He also rushed 18 times for 85 yards and two touchdowns, the 50th and 51st of his career, breaking a tie with Herschel Walker to become the SEC's all-time career leader for rushing touchdowns. Tebow said afterwards, "Breaking Herschel's record means a lot. Just to be mentioned in the same breath as Herschel Walker, it's extremely humbling and a little bit breathtaking because it's Herschel Walker. How am I going to be in the same league as Herschel Walker? I still can't understand it. It's pretty cool and it's really special."

Now for some trivia:

Question 280: Turnovers played a large part in this game. No turnovers for Florida's offense, a lot of picks for Florida's defense. How many times did Florida intercept a Georgia pass in this game?

a) 3
b) 4
c) 5
d) 6

Question 281: Florida's defense scored a touchdown for the second week in a row off an interception return. Which Florida defender returned an interception for a TD vs. Georgia?

a) Ryan Stamper
b) Carlos Dunlap
c) Brandon Spikes
d) Major Wright

Question 282: What is Florida's record in the last 20 meetings in this rivalry game?

a) 14-6
b) 15-5
c) 16-4
d) 17-3

Question 283: Who caught both of Tebow's first quarter TD passes to get the Gators off to a quick start?

a) Aaron Hernandez
b) Riley Cooper

c) Brandon James
d) Deonte Thompson

ANSWER KEY – GEORGIA

280. B – 4.

281. C – Brandon Spikes.

282. D – 17-3.

283. B – Riley Cooper.

VANDERBILT

"Have you ever gone 19-0? It's not ho-hum, I can assure you that. If it's ho-hum for someone, you've got to really reflect and say, 'Where am I headed in this life right now?' If 19-0 in the Southeastern Conference at the University of Florida is ho-hum, then you've got one exciting life, you've got a lot of good stuff going for you."

Those were the words of Coach Meyer after Florida won its home game vs. Vanderbilt, 27-3, to extend the school record and nation's longest winning streak to 19 games. The win also matched the fourth longest winning streak by an SEC team since 1960. Despite the relatively easy win, his words came in response to some tough questions about Florida's offense and what many described as a lackluster performance, especially coming on the heels of a dominating win vs. Georgia.

When the same questions were put to Tim Tebow after the game, he replied, "You'd like to put the ball in the end zone more and not kick field goals, but we're going to be happy being 9-0. Not too many teams in the country are 9-0."

As for why some were questioning the performance by the Gators offense, on its first possession Florida was three-and-out, taking just 16 seconds off the clock and gaining six yards before punting. On its second possession, Florida began on its own 15 and drove 75 yards on 13 plays, but then had to settle for a field goal to take a 3-0 lead. Florida finally got the ball into the end zone on its third possession, but stalled and settled for a field goal on its fourth possession, and then went three-and-out on its final possession of the first half. Still, the Gators led 13-0 at the half.

In five possessions in the second half, Florida found the end zone twice, but the Gators began the half with a three-and-out, later had a five-play drive that ended with a punt, and then on its last possession, Florida turned the ball over on downs as the offense tried to run out the clock.

The defense, as usual, was stellar – even without Brandon Spikes, who was suspended for the game after the "eye-poking" incident.

Key stats: Florida was only 4 for 13 on third down conversions, again, one of the reasons people pointed fingers at the Gators offense. Vanderbilt managed only 199 yards of total offense, while Tim Tebow passed for 208 yards and a touchdown.

Now for some trivia:

Question 284: Florida fans were a bit antsy, holding on to a 3-0 lead in the second quarter, wondering when the offense was going to bust one. The fans got something to cheer about when Florida broke a 25-yard run for the first TD of the game. Which Florida player gave the fans something to cheer about with his 25-yard touchdown?

a) Tim Tebow
b) Jeff Demps
c) Chris Rainey
d) Emmanuel Moody

Question 285: What is Florida's record vs. Vanderbilt over the past 19 games in which these two teams have played?

a) 19-0
b) 18-1
c) 17-2
d) 16-3

Question 286: Tebow was 15 for 20 passing, good for 208 yards – and 120 of those yards went to the same guy. Who led the Gators with 120 yards receiving vs. Vanderbilt?

a) Brandon James
b) Riley Cooper
c) Aaron Hernandez
d) David Nelson

Question 287: The Gators scored three touchdowns on the day. Which of the following players *did not* get into the end zone for Florida?

a) Tim Tebow
b) Jeff Demps
c) Aaron Hernandez
d) David Nelson

ANSWER KEY – VANDERBILT

284. B – Jeff Demps.

285. A – 19-0.

286. C – Aaron Hernandez.

287. C – Aaron Hernandez.

SOUTH CAROLINA

Jarvis Moss blocked a South Carolina field goal attempt as time expired in 2006 to preserve a 17-16 victory for Florida – one that enabled the club to play its way into the BCS National Championship Game. Three years later, it took another big defensive play for the Gators to hold off the Gamecocks. With Florida clinging to a 17-14 second half lead, South Carolina marched 49 yards on 11 plays to set up the potential go-ahead score before the Gators defense picked off a Stephen Garcia pass to end the threat.

After the pick it took the Gators offense just four plays to get into the end zone – capped by a one-yard TD run by Tim Tebow – and put the Gamecocks away, 24-14.

The victory gave the Gators a perfect season in the SEC for the first time since 1996, when Coach Spurrier was on the sidelines at Florida. As for the game itself, Coach Spurrier said it was "that turnover" that made the difference.

Coach Meyer said, "We did not play perfect . . . but that's 20 in a row and I'm awful proud of the guys in there."

Key stats: Florida's defense shut out the Gamecocks in the second half and gave up only 247 total yards for the game. South Carolina gained just 61 yards on the ground and was only 3 for 12 on third down conversions. Florida's defense also forced three turnovers, while the Gators offense did not turn the ball over at all. Tim Tebow scored his 53rd career touchdown, tying Kevin Faulk (who scored 53 combined rushing and receiving TDs for LSU) for the most in SEC history.

Now for some trivia:

Question 288: Florida got off to a quick start. The defense forced a three-and-out after South Carolina received the opening kick. And then the Gators offense went 86 yards on four plays on its opening drive thanks to a big touchdown play. Who caught a 68-yard touchdown pass from Tim Tebow to get the Gators on the board first?

a) Deonte Thompson

b) Riley Cooper

c) Aaron Hernandez
d) David Nelson

Question 289: Florida's second TD of the game came in the second quarter and put the Gators up 17-7. It was also the first TD of the year for this player . . . who was he?

a) Emmanuel Moody
b) Andre Debose
c) Justin Williams
d) T.J. Lawrence

Question 290: Who was the defensive player that made the game-changing interception in the second half for Florida?

a) Carlos Dunlap
b) Brandon Spikes
c) Justin Trattou
d) Major Wright

ANSWER KEY – SOUTH CAROLINA

288. B – Riley Cooper.

289. A – Emmanuel Moody.

290. C – Justin Trattou.

FIU

Florida got a break in its schedule the week before taking on in-state rival FSU, hosting the FIU Golden Panthers.

No real drama here. Florida won 62-3.

Florida improved its nation-best and school record winning streak to 21 games and for the second time in school history began a season with an 11-0 record.

Key stats: Tim Tebow was 17 for 25 passing, good for 215 yards and two touchdowns. Then John Brantley came on . . . and Brantley was 9 for 13 passing, good for 146 yards and *three* touchdowns.

Now for some trivia:

Question 291: Florida's defense scored the first points of the game. Who returned an interception 41 yards for a touchdown to get Florida on the board?

a) Carlos Dunlap
b) Major Wright
c) Brandon Spikes
d) Ahmad Black

Question 292: Florida also scored a touchdown on its first offensive possession. It was a rushing TD for Tim Tebow, the 54th of his career, breaking the SEC record for touchdowns held by Kevin Faulk. It was also the longest rushing TD of Tebow's career. How long was it?

a) 45 yards
b) 50 yards
c) 55 yards
d) 60 yards

Question 293: Florida scored nine touchdowns, but only one Gator made it into the end zone twice. Who scored two touchdowns vs. FIU?

a) Chris Rainey
b) Riley Cooper
c) Tim Tebow
d) Aaron Hernandez

Question 294: Which of the following players did not score a touchdown vs. FIU?

a) Chris Rainey
b) Riley Cooper
c) Justin Williams
d) Aaron Hernandez

ANSWER KEY – FIU

291. C – Brandon Spikes.

292. C – 55 yards.

293. A – Chris Rainey.

294. D – Aaron Hernandez.

FLORIDA STATE

Ron Zook and the 2004 Gators were the first team to win in Tallahassee since 1986, and FSU has not beaten Florida since – home or away. Florida closed out its 2009 regular season schedule with a home date against in-state rival FSU. The Gators came into the game having won a school record 21 straight games, including 15 consecutive SEC games, ten straight at home, and eight straight against non-conference opponents. Not to mention the five straight over FSU, beginning with that 2004 victory.

Ahmad Black spoke about the streak and the rivalry beforehand, saying, "There's a lot of hatred. It started even before us. It goes way back to the earlier days. We're just going to try to keep it going. We've won five straight, so we don't want to be the team that loses the streak."

College GameDay was in town – and it was also Senior Day, the final time Tim Tebow, Brandon Spikes and the rest of the 2009 Senior Class would play in The Swamp. Tens of thousands of fans showed their support for Tim Tebow by wearing black eye paint – some with scripture references used by Tebow in the past, others with Tebow's name and number. Tebow said of the gesture, "That was special."

After an emotional Gator Walk and an even more emotional ceremony honoring the seniors, it was time to play ball.

And boy did the Gators play ball.

Tebow connected with Aaron Hernandez for the first score of the game, and the Gators led 7-0 after the first quarter. It got ugly in the second quarter.

A field goal, followed by an 18-yard TD run by Tebow, and then another TD pass to Hernandez, and it was 24-0 at the half.

Florida led 30-0 before FSU managed a field goal.

The final score: 37-10.

Afterwards Coach Meyer said, "I don't want to say goodbye. The good thing is we're not done. The negative thing is we're done in this great stadium."

Key stats: Florida was 10 for 13 on third down conversions – FSU was just 2 for 11. Florida's offense tallied 545 total yards, compared to just 269 for FSU. Florida rushed for 311 yards, compared to just 83 for FSU.

Now for some trivia:

Question 295: Who was the leading rusher for the Gators with 106 yards on just seven carries?

a) Jeff Demps
b) Tim Tebow
c) Chris Rainey
d) Mike Gillislee

Question 296: How many total touchdowns did Tim Tebow account for vs. FSU (passing and rushing combined)?

a) 2
b) 3
c) 4
d) 5

Question 297: How many different players had at least one play of 25-plus yards for the Gators?

a) 4
b) 5
c) 6
d) 7

Question 298: How many different players had at least one play of 25-plus yards for the Seminoles?

a) 1
b) 2
c) 3
d) 4

Question 299: Which two Florida defenders both intercepted a pass vs. FSU?

a) Joe Haden and Adrian Bushnell
b) Carlos Dunlap and Brandon Spikes
c) Major Wright and Ahmad Black
d) Ryan Stamper and Dustin Doe

ANSWER KEY – FLORIDA STATE

295. A – Jeff Demps.

296. D – 5.

297. C – 6.

298. A – 1.

299. A – Joe Haden and Adrian Bushnell.

ALABAMA

And then it was over. Florida's best-in-the-nation and school record winning streak, SEC winning streak, and quest for perfection came to an end in the SEC Championship Game vs. Alabama, 32-13. It was a rematch of 2008, No. 1 vs. No. 2 – only this time the roles were reversed. It was a matchup that TV executives and fans all over the country had been drooling over since a year earlier, when the Gators rallied for two late touchdowns to win the SEC Championship and a berth in the BCS National Championship Game – unfortunately, there was no fourth-quarter comeback this time around.

Joe Haden said afterwards, "They seemed like they wanted it a whole lot." Tim Tebow added, "It's tough. You know it's not how you want to go out. They were just better than us today."

Alabama got off to a quick start in the first quarter, taking a 9-0 lead. After trading field goals to make it 12-3, Tebow connected with David Nelson on a 23-yard touchdown pass to close within two, 12-10. The next series was perhaps the biggest in the game. Alabama had received the ball to open the half, and Florida would get the ball to start the second half. With only 3:32 left on the clock and a two-point deficit, if Florida's defense could get a stop and get the team into the locker room down only two at the half, Florida's offense would have a chance to take the lead with its opening drive in the second half. Unfortunately, a short pass to Mark Ingram that looked like it might go for a loss turned into a 69-yard gain thanks to a missed tackle. It was just one more spectacular play for Ingram on the finest day of his career. The very next play, Ingram ran it in for a touchdown and a 19-10 lead. The Gators managed a field goal before the half to make it 19-13, but the offense was unable to do anything with its opening drive in the third quarter.

The Gators went three-and-out to start the second half – and Florida's offense only touched the ball four times in the second half, ran just 23 plays, and scored zero points. Four possessions: punt, punt, interception, and turnover on downs. The interception was crucial because it came on a goal-to-go situation after the Gators drove 59 yards on seven plays, but the truth is the Tide had already scored 14 unanswered points and the Gators still would have trailed by two scores.

Key stats: Alabama's running game allowed the Tide to dominate time of possession: 251 rushing yards (the most ever for a team against the Gators since Urban Meyer took over as Head Coach) and 39:37, compared to 88 rushing yards and 20:23 for the Gators. Mark Ingram's performance earned him the Heisman Trophy – he finished the game with three touchdowns and 189 total yards. Other key stats that illustrate how Alabama controlled this game so thoroughly: the Tide was 11 for 15 on third down conversions, Florida was only 4 for 11; the Tide had one penalty for five yards, Florida had five penalties for 51 yards; and the Tide won the turnover battle – none for Alabama, one for Florida.

Now for some trivia:

Question 300: It was only the second time since Coach Meyer came to Florida that a team ran for more than 200 yards against the Gators. The previous high was 247. Which team beat Florida in 2007 after gaining 247 yards on the ground?

a) Alabama
b) LSU
c) Georgia
d) Arkansas

Question 301: Florida's defense came into the game ranked #1 in the country, giving up fewer than ten points per game while allowing on average just 233 total yards per game. How many total yards did Florida's defense give up to Alabama?

a) 480
b) 490
c) 500
d) 510

Question 302: Who was the leading receiver for the Gators with 85 yards on eight catches?

a) Aaron Hernandez
b) Riley Cooper
c) David Nelson
d) Deonte Thompson

Question 303: Who was the Alabama defensive back that made the big interception of a Tebow pass in the end zone?

a) DeMarcus DuBose
b) Courtney Upshaw
c) Javier Arenas
d) Justin Woodall

Question 304: Who was the leading rusher for the Gators with 63 yards on ten carries?

a) Tim Tebow
b) Brandon James
c) Jeff Demps
d) Chris Rainey

ANSWER KEY – ALABAMA

300. B – LSU.

301. B – 490.

302. A – Aaron Hernandez.

303. C – Javier Arenas.

304. A – Tim Tebow.

CINCINNATI

Florida's loss to Alabama was devastating, but even with the turmoil of Coach Meyer's retirement-un-retirement-leave-of-absence flurry in the days leading up to the Sugar Bowl there was this overwhelming sense that somebody was going to have to pay for that loss, and that somebody was going to be Cincinnati – the No. 3 ranked team in the country and the Gators opponent in New Orleans.

Cincinnati was undefeated, Big East Champs, and looking for a chance to prove it belonged in a game against a Florida-caliber team.

Well, not this time.

This one was over, fast.

The Gators scored first, and often, building a 23-0 lead before the Bearcats kicked a 47-yard field goal late in the first half. Florida came right back with a touchdown to make it 30-3 at the half.

The final score: 51-24.

"It was incredible. Just a great game," Tim Tebow said. "It was exactly how you want to go out with these seniors and these coaches in your last game and your last time together. It just really doesn't get any better than this."

Tebow's final performance as a Gator was his finest – his teammate Carl Johnson said, "They couldn't stop Superman. They needed some kryptonite." The Gators offense, led by Tebow, scored on its first five possessions and never looked back.

Cincinnati and quarterback Tony Pike came into the game with a high-scoring offense, but Florida's defense was more than up for the task. The Bearcats managed only 19 total yards of offense in the first quarter, compared to 152 yards for the Gators. Florida led 44-10 after three quarters, and it was only a pair of fourth quarter touchdowns – after the game was well out of reach – that kept the 51-24 final from being even worse.

"I didn't see this coming, but I knew we had a great game plan," said Tebow. Brandon Spikes added, "That game in Atlanta hurt. I told the guys we would get another opportunity to play like we know how to play, and I think we did that today."

Key stats: Florida had 12 penalties for 90 yards . . . but it didn't matter. Florida was 6 for 12 on third down conversions, Cincinnati was 4 for 15 – but both teams got it done on fourth down. Florida was 2 for 2 and Cincinnati was 3 for 3 on fourth down conversions. Cincinnati's high-powered offense was limited to just 246 total yards by Florida's defensive unit. The Gators improved to 13-1 on the season – becoming the first team in the Football Bowl Subdivision to win 13 games in consecutive seasons.

Now for some trivia:

Question 305: Tim Tebow was on *fire* when this game started. How many consecutive completions did Tebow record to start the game?

a) 9
b) 10
c) 11
d) 12

Question 306: And Tebow never let up either. He was 17 for 18 passing in the first half. How many yards and how many touchdowns did Tebow pass for in the *first half*?

a) 285 yards, one touchdown
b) 290 yards, two touchdowns
c) 295 yards, three touchdowns
d) 305 yards, four touchdowns

Question 307: Tebow was 31 for 35 passing for the game and he also set a couple of career highs – including one for most yards passing. How many yards passing did Tebow have for the game?

a) 472
b) 482
c) 492
d) 502

Question 308: The other career high for Tebow was an 80-yard touchdown pass. Who was on the receiving end of this career-best throw?

a) Riley Cooper
b) Aaron Hernandez
c) Deonte Thompson
d) David Nelson

Question 309: And yet another record for Tebow . . . he broke Vince Young's BCS bowl record for most total yards in a game. Young had 467 combined passing and rushing yards in the 2005 Rose Bowl. How many total yards did Tebow have vs. Cincinnati?

a) 513
b) 523
c) 533
d) 543

Question 310: Who was the leading rusher for the Gators with 78 yards on just five carries?

a) Mike Gillislee
b) Chris Rainey
c) Emmanuel Moody
d) Jeff Demps

Question 311: Florida had four rushing touchdowns. Which of the following *did not* get into the end zone on the ground?

a) Tim Tebow
b) Chris Rainey
c) Emmanuel Moody
d) Mike Gillislee

Question 312: Who was the leading receiver for the Gators with 181 yards on seven catches?

a) Riley Cooper
b) Aaron Hernandez
c) Deonte Thompson
d) David Nelson

Question 313: Florida had four players with at least 60 receiving yards – and three of them got into the end zone as well. Which of the following *did not* get into the end zone through the air?

a) Riley Cooper
b) Aaron Hernandez
c) Deonte Thompson
d) Chris Rainey

Question 314: How many total points did Florida kicker Caleb Sturgis record (field goals plus PATs)?

a) 8
b) 9
c) 10
d) 11

Question 315: Florida had 11 offensive possessions. How many times did Florida punter Chas Henry have to boot the ball away?

a) 0
b) 1
c) 2
d) 3

ANSWER KEY – CINCINNATI

305. D – 12.

306. C – 295 yards, three touchdowns.

307. B – 482.

308. A – Riley Cooper.

309. C – 533.

310. A – Mike Gillislee.

311. D – Mike Gillislee.

312. A – Riley Cooper.

313. D – Chris Rainey.

314. B – 9.

315. B – 1.

ABOUT THE AUTHOR

LARRY HORNE grew up in the Gainesville area, played three sports at P K Yonge High School in Gainesville, and graduated in 1962. After three years in the Army, he graduated from the University of Florida in 1971 with a degree from the College of Journalism and Communications. He is a corporate communications manager of an electric utility. He married Connie Walden of Charleston, SC in 1968. Their three sons are all married and the Horne's have three grandchildren – all Gators-to-be, of course.

ACKNOWLEDGEMENTS

ON A PERSONAL NOTE …

I have been particularly blessed with a great family. Special thanks to my wife, Connie, for her full support in writing this book, and to my sons, Dwin, David, and Benji, for their love and support throughout the years. While sports have played a role in our lives, it's been my family's faith that I am most proud.

Thanks also to my friend Rick Anderson of Gainesville, Florida for his research and kindness in providing information from his collection of Gator memorabilia. Rick's Vintage Collectibles is on the Internet, so look him up: http://ricka30327.com/home

My memories of the Florida Gators date back to the early '50s. Selling cokes in the stands during the first half, then watching the rest of the game the second half. I would go home and wrap up newspapers. I would then put them under my t-shirt to give the appearance of shoulder pads. Then, I would pretend I was a Gator. One of my favorite players was Jimmy Rountree.

Insofar as game memories, I recall seeing Bobby Joe Green's 82-yard-punt against Georgia in 1958, the famed Florida-Georgia Tech game that the Gators won 18-17 in 1960; the first Florida-FSU game in 1958 and many others, including the John Reaves-Carlos Alvarez 70-yarder.

And, of course, I want to mention my lifelong Gainesville best friends – Ted Douglas, Jim Weber and Harry Allen. Ted was certainly the best athlete in our school, Jim was the smartest and Harry is a much better journalist. They're special friends and big fans of the Gators. They grew up right along with me. Thanks guys for being my lifelong best friends.

REFERENCES

APPollArchive.com – The AP Poll Archive website
CNNSI.com
ESPN.com
Gamecocksonline.cstv.com – The official website of University of South Carolina Athletics
GatorZone.com – The official website of University of Florida Athletics
Heisman.com – The official Heisman Trophy website
NFL.com – The official website of the NFL
NFL.com/draft – The official NFL Draft website
Ricka30327.com – Rick Anderson of Gainesville, FL (Rick's Vintage Collectibles)
RollTide.com – The official website of University of Alabama Athletics
SECsports.com – The official website of the Southeastern Conference
University of Alabama Media Guide (2009)
University of Florida Media Guide (2008 and 2009)
University of South Carolina Media Guide (2009)

ABOUT BLACK MESA

Look for these titles in the popular Trivia IQ Series:

Atlanta Braves
New York Yankees
Tampa Bay Rays
Cincinnati Reds
Cleveland Indians
Baltimore Orioles
Boston Red Sox (Volumes (I & II)
Milwaukee Brewers
St. Louis Cardinals (Volumes I & II)
Major League Baseball
Mixed Martial Arts (Volumes I & II)
Boston Celtics (Volumes I & II)
University of Florida Gators Football
University of Georgia Bulldogs Football
University of Oklahoma Sooners Football
University of Texas Longhorns Football
Texas A&M Aggies Football
West Point Football
New England Patriots
Buffalo Bills
Kentucky Derby
NHL Hockey
Rock & Roll
The Beatles

Look for these titles in the Sports by the Numbers Series:

Major League Baseball
New York Yankees
Boston Red Sox
San Francisco Giants
Atlanta Braves
Texas Rangers
University of Oklahoma Football
University of Georgia Football
Penn State Football
NASCAR
Sacramento Kings Basketball
Mixed Martial Arts